CHARLES LAMB AND THE THEATRE

CHARLES LAMB
AND THE THEATRE

Wayne McKenna

COLIN SMYTHE
Gerrards Cross 1978

First published in 1978 by Colin Smythe Limited
Gerrards Cross, Buckinghamshire

ISBN 0–901072–61–3

Set by Watford Typesetters Ltd.
and printed and bound by Billing & Sons Ltd.,
Guildford, London and Worcester
Produced in Great Britain

Contents

Acknowledgements   6

Introduction   7

I   English Theatre 1737-1843   19

II   Lamb as Critic of Dramatic Literature   37

III   Lamb as Dramatist   55

IV   Lamb as Critic of Theatrical Performance   73

V   Lamb as Critic of Shakespeare   97

Notes   121

Acknowledgements

I am indebted to many friends and colleagues who have assisted me in various parts of this book. I express my especial thanks to Professor J. E. Morpurgo who first stimulated my interest in Lamb and who constantly advised and encouraged me during the writing of this work. I also thank Professor A. Hardie and Mr W. C. Chan for their constructive criticisms, and Professor A. N. Jeffares for his many kindnesses and encouragement.

I am grateful to Mrs Marie Hill who typed for me with wonderful patience and proficiency.

I thank the editors of *English Studies* and *The Charles Lamb Bulletin* for permission to use material which has appeared in those journals.

I am most grateful to my wife, Bernadette, for her unfailing support.

Introduction

Many critical comments on Lamb stress the gentleness and the whimsicality of his character and writing and often lead to a patronising dismissal of his importance. Klingopulos wrote of him as a 'fairly simple, friendly man' and added that 'Critical comments about Lamb often become inventive or evasive, primarily because there is a disproportion between the legend and the actual literary achievement'.[1] Such judgements misrepresent Lamb because they do not sufficiently respect the essential seriousness of his criticism and because they ignore his strength of mind. His comments on contemporary poets and poetry, his political lampoons, and his quarrels with Coleridge and Southey reveal both his insight and his pungent frankness, and those qualities of unflinching honesty which marked this writing also characterized his criticism of dramatic literature and the theatre. Lamb wrestled with unorthodox and paradoxical arguments not, as Howe suggested, because he had a 'strain of perverseness . . . which led him sometimes to unreasonable extremes',[2] but because he abhorred facile conclusions and never shirked the implications of his ideas. His criticism includes no 'baroque whimsicalities' despite the allegation by Wimsatt and Brooks that these exist even in the criticism on Shakespeare.[3] Lamb's comments upon Shakespeare and the theatre derived partly from principles of criticism which were fundamental to his approach to painting as well as to poetry and drama. He raised the important aesthetic issue of the potential of stage performances of poetic drama.

This book will discuss the predominant characteristics of English theatre during the period 1737–1843, from the application of the 'Licensing Act' until its revocation, and it will comment on Lamb as dramatist, as critic of dramatic literature, as critic and experiencer of theatrical performance, and as critic of Shakespeare and painting. De Quincey argued that Lamb had 'the dramatic intellect and taste, perhaps in perfection', and this ability distinguished his criticism.[4] The notes to the *Specimens of English Dramatic Poets* and the *Extracts from the Garrick Plays* reveal principles of criticism which are essential to any

assessment of Lamb as a critic. In his essays on theatrical performance, his ideas on acting generated his defence of 'artificial
comedy' against the conventional charge of immorality. He progressively elaborated a theory of the significance of acting
techniques in determining dramatic illusion and audience
response, and in his comments on actors like Bensley, Dodd,
Munden, Fanny Kelly, and Mrs Jordan he developed an implicit
contrast between 'artificial' and 'natural' acting.[5] His awareness
of the different effects which these techniques could produce
formed the basis of the essays on 'Stage Illusion' and 'On the
Artificial Comedy of the Last Century', and enabled him to con-
clude that if 'artificial comedy' were acted with the appropriate
technique then the audience would not consider the play immoral.
All of this, together with the essay on Shakespeare, combined to
form a serious group of critical essays and not a series of
aberrations.

Something of the actor existed in Lamb's very character, and
his 'dramatic intellect and taste' appeared not only in his writing
on theatre but also in his Elian essays. In a letter to Fanny Kelly
on 20 July 1819, in which he proposed marriage, he wrote:

> In many a sweet assumed character I have learned to love
> you, but simply as F. M. Kelly I love you better than them all.
> Can you quit these shadows of existence, & come & be a
> reality to us? can you leave off harassing yourself to please a
> thankless multitude, who know nothing of you, & begin at last
> to live to yourself & your friends?
>
> As plainly & frankly as I have seen you give or refuse assent
> in some feigned scene, so frankly do me the justice to answer
> me.[6]

The character of Elia provided him with the 'assumed character'
and those 'shadows of existence' in which he saw Fanny Kelly
when she acted on the stage. He adopted the persona of Elia and
a dramatic element characterized his own account of Elian self-
projection, since Elia could 'imply and twine with his own
identity the griefs and affections of another – making himself
many, or reducing many unto himself'. As Elia, Lamb created
an idiosyncratic blend of biographical fact and fiction, of truth,
half-truth, and the blatant lie. Elia was Lamb's most candid
biographer but he remained the least reliable. In the voice of a
'Friend of the Late Elia' Lamb acknowledged that what Elia 'tells

us, as of himself, was often true only (historically) of another; as in a former Essay . . . where under the *first person* (his favourite figure) he shadows forth the forlorn estate of a country-boy placed at a London school, far from his friends and connections – in direct opposition to his own early history'.[7] This referred to the essay 'Christ's Hospital Five and Thirty Years Ago' in which Elia adopted the persona of Coleridge. If those events lacked historical truth they nevertheless embodied an imaginative truth. Lamb could realize this truth by a process of sympathetic identification, and this process characterized his theatrical response.[8] As Robert Frank recently suggested, Lamb remained aware, both in his Elian essays and in his comments on the theatre, of the distinction between 'an aesthetic experience and other modes of consciousness – ethical, practical, or critical'.[9]

Lamb was an avid playgoer with strikingly catholic tastes. He enjoyed serious drama but he also relished the most unpretentious entertainment. In a letter to Dorothy Wordsworth of 9 July 1803 Mary Lamb described a visit to Sadler's Wells 'the lowest and most London-like of all our London amusements – the entertainments were Goody Two Shoes, Jack the Giant Killer, and *Mary of Buttermere!*' and Charles 'laughed the whole time' (*Letters*, I, 353). He appreciated many aspects of the theatre, and he also enjoyed the company of those associated with it. His circle of friends included Liston, Elliston, Charles Mathews, Sheridan Knowles, Kenney, J. H. Payne, Henry Robertson (treasurer of Covent Garden), Miss Burrell, Macready, Charles Kemble, Fanny Kelly, and Munden. Talfourd wrote that on the night of Munden's last performance on the London stage, in the interval between the play and the farce, Munden handed a porter pot to Lamb who was seated near the stage.[10] This gesture reflected the sympathy which existed between Lamb and actors.

II

A study which includes an assessment of Lamb's critical abilities demands clarification of the concept of the allegedly 'gentle' Elia. Lamb vigorously rejected the description of him as 'gentle-hearted' which Coleridge included in his poem 'This Lime-Tree Bower my Prison':

> For God's sake (I never was more serious), don't make me
> ridiculous any more by terming me gentle-hearted in print, or
> do it in better verses. It did well enough five years ago when
> I came to see you, and was moral coxcomb enough at the time
> you wrote the lines, to feed upon such epithets; but, besides
> that, the meaning of gentle is equivocal at best, and almost
> always means poor-spirited, the very quality of gentleness is
> abhorrent to such vile trumpetings. My *sentiment* is long since
> vanished. I hope my *virtues* have done *sucking*. I can scarce
> think but you meant it in joke. I hope you did, for I should
> be ashamed to think that you could think to gratify me by such
> praise, fit only to be a cordial to some green-sick sonneteer.
> (*Letters,* I, 198).

Lamb clearly stated his seriousness. He accurately foresaw the
negative and patronising implications which accompanied
Coleridge's rather clumsy comment. When Lamb used the term
'gentle' himself, in his note on Heywood's *Fortune by Land and
Sea* in the *Extracts from the Garrick Plays,* he elucidated his
meaning with care:

> in all those qualities which gained for Shakspeare the attribute
> of *gentle,* he was not inferior to him. Generosity, courtesy,
> temperance in the depths of passion; sweetness, in a word, and
> gentleness; Christianism; and true hearty Anglicism of feelings,
> shaping that Christianism; shine throughout his beautiful writ-
> ings in a manner more conspicuous than in those of
> Shakspeare, but only more conspicuous, inasmuch as in
> Heywood these qualities are primary, in the other subordinate
> to poetry. I love them both equally, but Shakspeare has most
> of my wonder. (IV, 419).

The quality of gentleness, as Lamb here described it, did not
suggest poor-spirited and it contrasted with the allegedly 'vile
trumpetings' of Coleridge's poem. The validity and the tone of
some of the comments with which Lamb reproached Coleridge
dispel notions of a weak Lamb.

Lamb could write unflinchingly honest criticism, and this
appeared in his comments upon the poetry of Coleridge,
Wordsworth, and Southey. These comments appeared in his
correspondence with these authors, in which he regularly recorded
his reactions to their work. He criticized freely and spontaneously
and he earnt their respect for his judgements. To Coleridge he

would admit his errors (' I believe I was wrong in most of my other objections'), but he could also stand firm: 'But surely "hailed him immortal", adds nothing to the terror of the man's death, which it was your business to heighten, not diminish by a phrase which takes away all terror from it' (*Letters,* I, 100). On occasions he commented severely; and he parodied Coleridge's 'Dactyls' in a letter of June 1796 (*Letters,* I, 32). This irritated Coleridge, and on 6 July Lamb wrote: 'For your Dactyls I am sorry you are so sore about 'em – a very Sir Fretful! In good troth, the Dactyls are good Dactyls, but their measure is naught' (*Letters,* I, 37). He refused to recant. Between 1796–8 Lamb proposed numerous amendments to Coleridge's poems, and Coleridge valued these comments. In a letter to Cottle of 6 January 1797 he wrote of 'sending my Visions of the Maid Of Arc & my correcting of the Joan of Arc, to Wordsworth . . . & to *Lamb,* whose *taste* & *judgement* I see reason to think more correct & philosophical than my own, which yet I place pretty high'. To Godwin Coleridge wrote on 21 May 1800 that 'Lamb every now & then *eradiates,* & the beam, tho' single & fine as a hair, yet is rich with colours, & I both see & feel it'. Lamb's 'taste acts so as to appear like the unmechanic simplicity of an Instinct'.[11] This showed a profound respect for Lamb's ability as a critic of literature, and Coleridge was not the least judge of such ability.

Lamb's criticisms frequently revolved around his perception of what he described to Coleridge in February 1797 as a 'certain faulty disproportion in the matter and the *style* (*Letters,* I, 98). Wordsworth sought to avoid exactly this kind of criticism when in the Preface to the *Lyrical Ballads* he hoped 'that my ideas are expressed in language fitted to their respective importance'.[12] In another letter to Coleridge in June 1796 Lamb objected to some of Southey's personifications in *Joan of Arc* because 'they are not very striking and only encumber', and he added that 'all the passage about Love . . . is very confused and sickens me with a load of useless personifications' (*Letters,* I, 14). Coleridge perhaps replied to these comments by listing personifications to which Lamb's criticism did not apply, for subsequently Lamb wrote: 'To your list of illustrative personifications, into which a fine imagination enters, I will take leave to add the following from Beaumont and Fletcher's "Wife for a Month"' (*Letters,* I, 28).

11

Lamb rejected personification not in an absolute sense but only when it disrupted the unity of the poem by its irrelevance. Wordsworth rejected personification for the same reason when in the Preface to the *Lyrical Ballads* he claimed that he would avoid personification 'as a mechanical device of style'.[13] Lamb wanted Coleridge to write with greater strength and clarity, and his proposed alterations to the 'Monody on Chatterton', for instance, aimed to 'make it more compress'd and I think more energic' (*Letters,* I, 17). In November 1796 he urged Coleridge: 'Cultivate simplicity, Coleridge, or rather, I should say, banish elaborateness; for simplicity springs spontaneous from the heart, and carries into daylight its own modest buds and genuine, sweet, and clear flowers of expression. I allow no hot-beds in the gardens of Parnassus' (*Letters,* I, 55–6). In these comments he advocated principles which four years later Wordsworth incorporated into his Preface. Lamb's comments bear a striking similarity to Wordsworth's phrases 'simple and unelaborated expressions' and 'spontaneous overflow of powerful feelings',[14] which formed a centrally important part of his critical ideas on poetry. Lamb arrived at these ideas uninfluenced by Wordsworth. He had an independent mind.

In the letters in which he discussed Coleridge's poetry Lamb also commented upon his character. He argued that in some of the letters where Coleridge talked 'in a religious strain' he adopted 'a certain freedom of expression, a certain air of mysticism, more consonant to the conceits of pagan philosophy, than consistent with the humility of genuine piety' (*Letters,* I, 48). Lamb wrote that he found this offensive, and amongst the examples of what he referred to he quoted from the letter which Coleridge had written to him immediately after Mary Lamb's matricide. Coleridge had stated: 'You are a temporary sharer in human misery, that you may be an eternal partaker of the Divine Nature.' Lamb commented:

What more than this do those men say, who are for exalting the man Christ Jesus into the second person of an unknown Trinity, – men, whom you or I scruple not to call idolaters? Man, full of imperfections, at best, and subject to wants which momentarily remind him of dependence; man, a weak and ignorant being, 'servile' from his birth 'to all the skiey influences', with eyes sometimes open to discern the right path, but a head generally too dizzy to pursue it; man, in the pride of speculation, forgetting his nature, and hailing in himself the future God, must make the angels laugh. Be not angry with me, Coleridge; I wish not to cavil; I know I cannot *instruct* you; I only wish to *remind* you of that humility which best becometh the Christian character. (*Letters,* I, 49).

Lamb sent this to Coleridge on 24 October 1796. Coleridge replied swiftly, and Lamb wrote again on 28 October:

My dear Friend, I am not ignorant that to be a partaker of the Divine Nature is a phrase to be met with in Scripture: I am only apprehensive, lest we in these latter days, tinctured (some of us perhaps pretty deeply) with mystical notions and the pride of metaphysics, might be apt to affix to such phrases a meaning, which the primitive users of them, the simple fishermen of Galilee for instance, never intended to convey. (*Letters,* 1, 50).

Lamb urged Coleridge to be less proud.

His readiness to believe in Coleridge's arrogance fired his impassioned outburst against him in 1798. He sent a series of *Theses Quaedam Theologicae* to Coleridge, and he included such questions as 'Whether the higher order of Seraphim Illuminati ever sneer?' (*Letters,* I, 123). He felt deeply offended by a comment allegedly made by Coleridge, and subsequently reported to him by Charles Lloyd, that if he wanted any knowledge he could write to Coleridge. Lamb could not tolerate anything which seemed like a betrayal of friendship. In 1823 he published a savage attack on Southey in a 'Letter of Elia to Robert Southey, Esq.', which appeared in *The London Magazine* of October 1823, when he felt that Southey had violated the responsibilities of friendship. In an article in the *Quarterly Review* of January 1823 entitled 'The Progress of Infidelity' Southey described the *Essays of Elia* as 'a book which wants only a sounder religious feeling, to be as delightful as it is original'. Lamb exploded in wrath, and he criticized the writings and character of Southey whom he styled the 'self-elected Court Poet to Beëlzebub' (I, 228). Lamb's own loyalty to his friends emerged in contrast to the actions of which he accused Southey: 'In more than one place, if I mistake not, you have been pleased to compliment me at the expence of my companions. I cannot accept your compliment at such a price' (I, 229). Lamb defended his friends Hazlitt and

Leigh Hunt whom he described as 'two gentlemen, diametrically opposed to yourself in principles' (I, 230). An irony existed in Southey's earlier comment in a letter to Coleridge in 1804 that there was 'not a man in the world who could so well revenge himself' as Lamb.[15] Southey apologized and Lamb replied that his wrath had partly stemmed from another statement by the *Quarterly Review* 'of its own knowledge, that the "Confessions of a Drunkard" was a genuine description of the state of the writer' (*Letters*, II, 407). The *Quarterly Review* had also angered Lamb in October 1814 by its alterations to his review of Wordsworth's *The Excursion*, and in 1811 by Gifford's reference to Lamb's comments on Ford (in the *Specimens*) as the 'blasphemies of a poor maniac'[16] – thus alluding to Lamb's six weeks confinement in the mental institution at Hoxton. This attack on Southey showed the ungentle side of Elia's character.

Lamb could be spiteful. In his few comments on Byron and Shelley he expressed an extreme contempt for these poets. On the death of Shelley he jested that 'Shelley the great Atheist has gone down by water to eternal fire!' (*Letters*, II, 333), and he referred to Bernard Barton's 'Verses on the Death of P. B. Shelley' as follows: 'I do not think it will convert the club at Pisa, neither do I think it will satisfy the bigots on our side the water. Something like a parody on the song of Ariel would please them better. "Full fathom five the Atheist lies,/Of his bones are hell-dice made"' (*Letters*, II, 338). Lamb detested the characters of both Byron and Shelley. He admitted that he had a 'thorough aversion' (*Letters*, II, 279) to Byron, and with reference to Southey's 'Vision of Judgment' he argued that to 'award his Heaven and his Hell in the presumptuous manner he has done, was a piece of immodesty as bad as Shelleyism' (*Letters*, II, 338). These personal criticisms combined with his objections to the nature of their poetry. He drew comparisons with Wordsworth and Shakespeare in order to emphasize the weaknesses of Byron and Shelley. Lamb thought that Byron was 'great in so little a way – To be a Poet is to be The Man, the whole Man – not a petty portion of occasional low passion worked up into a permanent form of Humanity. Shakespeare has thrust such rubbishly feelings into a corner, the dark dusty heart of Don John in the much Ado' (*Letters*, II, 279). He also believed that whereas 'a line of Wordsworth's is a lever to lift the immortal spirit! Byron

can only move the Spleen. He was at best a Satyrist, – in any
other way he was mean enough' (*Letters,* II, 426). As poet Byron
remained inferior to Wordsworth and Shakespeare because he
was more limited. Talfourd wrote that for Lamb 'all the Laras,
and Giaours, and Childe Harolds, were . . . "unreal mockeries", –
the phantasms of a feverish dream, – forms which did not appeal
to the sympathy of mankind, and never can find root among
them'.[17] In the essay on the 'Sanity of True Genius' Lamb had
argued that 'the true poet dreams being awake' (II, 187), and that
whilst the lesser poet 'turns life into a dream' the true poet 'to
the wildest dreams gives the sobrieties of every day occurrences'
(II, 189). Byron did not write like Lamb's 'true poet', and if
Talfourd recorded Lamb accurately then Lamb's judgement of
'phantasms of a feverish dream' suggested that ephemerality and
superficiality characterized some of Byron's work. As Lamb wrote
to Coleridge, he did not allow 'hot-beds in the gardens of
Parnassus', and this could apply to Shelley too, for Lamb declared
that Shelley's 'theories and nostrums . . . are oracular enough,
but I either comprehend 'em not, or there is miching malice and
mischief in 'em. But for the most part ringing with their own
emptiness. Hazlitt said well of 'em – Many are wiser and better
for reading Shakspeare, but nobody was ever wiser or better for
reading Sh—y' (*Letters,* II, 437). Lamb's social gatherings were
characterized by 'unpretending good sense'[18] and he did not
appreciate the visionary speculation of Shelley. He regarded it as
shallow. He had urged Coleridge to abandon the 'unsimple and
artificial' (*Letters,* I, 100), and he forcefully reproached his
abstraction. He argued that 'Good poetry' could not arise from
an 'unintelligible abstraction-fit', – which was how he characterized those lines in 'This Lime-tree Bower my Prison' where
Coleridge treated 'the manner of the Deity's making spirits perceive his presence. God, nor created thing alive, can receive any
honour from such thin show-box attributes' (*Letters,* I, 203).

The least distinguished and the most unpleasant aspect of
Lamb's criticism appeared in his political satires. One of the
ugliest attacks was levelled at Sir James Mackintosh of whom he
wrote:

> Though thou'rt like Judas, an apostate black,
> In the resemblance one thing thou dost lack:
> When he had gotten his ill-purchased pelf,

15

He went away, and wisely hanged himself.
This thou may'st do at last; yet much I doubt,
If thou hast any *bowels* to gush out! (V, 102).

The Albion, the newspaper to which he contributed this verse in
August 1801, soon failed. He informed Manning in a letter of
31 August 1801 that he had prospects of a post with the *Morning
Chronicle* and he added that this would require him to change
his tone: 'Mister Perry, in common with the great body of the
Whigs, thinks 'The Albion' *very low.* I find I must rise a peg or
so, be a little more decent and less abusive; for, to confess the
truth, I had arrived to an abominable pitch; I spared neither age
nor sex when my cue was given me' (*Letters,* I, 266). On 15 March
1812 Lamb's best known political satire appeared when Leigh
Hunt's *The Examiner* printed his attack on the Prince Regent.
This poem, which Lamb entitled 'The Triumph of the Whale',
attacked the Prince as well as his associates.

But about his presence keep
All the Monsters of the Deep;
Mermaids, with their tails and singing
His delighted fancy stinging;
Crooked Dolphins, they surround him,
Dog-like Seals, they fawn around him,
Following hard, the progress mark
Of the intolerant salt sea shark . . .
Hapless mariners are they,
Who beguil'd (as seamen say),
Deeming him some rock or island,
Footing sure, safe spot, and dry land,
Anchor in his scaly rind;
Soon the difference they find;
Sudden plumb, he sinks beneath them;
Does to ruthless seas bequeath them.   (V, 103–4)

Leigh Hunt spent the two years 1812–14 in prison for his responsibility for similar attacks on the Prince Regent.

In the years 1819–20 Lamb produced another series of
malicious criticisms. In *The Examiner* of 3–4 October 1819 he
criticized Gifford, and in 1820 he published several attacks in
The Champion. His victims included Canning and Castlereagh,
the government spies Castles, Oliver, and Edwards, and the king

himself. His hate for the Prince Regent, now George IV, had not diminished, and he wrote this poem entitled 'The Godlike':

> In one great man we view with odds
> A parallel to all the gods.
> Great Jove, that shook heaven with his brow,
> Could never match his princely bow.
> In him a Bacchus we behold:
> Like Bacchus, too, he ne'er grows old.
> Like Phoebus next, a flaming lover;
> And then he's Mercury – all over.
> A Vulcan, for domestic strife,
> He lamely lives without his wife.
> And sure – unless our wits be dull –
> Minerva-like, when moon was full,
> He issued from paternal skull.   (V, 104–5)

The last lines alluded to the alleged insanity of George III, and this comment showed a viciousness not totally dissimilar to Gifford's reference to Lamb as a 'poor maniac'. Lamb quarrelled rarely but he quarrelled ferociously. For the most part his sympathy and his humanity led him to reconciliation, but when he could not be reconciled, when his sense of justice was outraged and his anger aroused, he could be a savage commentator.

I English Theatre 1737-1843

i

Lamb's plays and his criticism of dramatic literature and theatrical performance not surprisingly relate to theatrical conditions during his lifetime. He worked at a time when the Licensing Act restricted theatrical activity in London so that only Drury Lane and Covent Garden held a 'Royal Patent' which permitted them to produce 'legitimate' drama. This law endured from 1737 until 1843, although theatres could evade its censorship by including music in their programmes. When Garrick acted at the unlicensed theatre in Goodman's Fields in 1741 the manager advertised a 'concert of vocal and instrumental music', and in the interval the play *Richard III* was produced gratis. This period from 1737-1843 produced many great actors but only two great dramatists, Sheridan and Goldsmith, and my comments on managers, actors, audiences, and dramatists will depict the theatrical conditions which generated this situation and provide a context for Lamb's interest in theatre.

J. J. Lynch pointed out that the manager of the patent theatres became a royal servant and was expected to bow to royal commands. Tate Wilkinson claimed that 'the patentees of Drury-Lane and Covent-Garden, not only go publicly to Court at St James's, but if they were to neglect that ceremony, at least occasionally, as on birth-days, &c. it would be taken notice of, judged a remissness, and not respectful'.[1] The patentee's duties extended beyond merely professional matters. Garrick, whose correspondence provides an invaluable source of information on the theatrical conditions of the period, found himself compelled to obey royal commands irrespective of the inconvenience which they might involve. He wrote to Charles Yorke in 1766: 'I am afraid that all of the boxes are taken for tomorrow, when by order of the Duke of York I shall be oblig'd to Act a Character, not well suited to my time of life, which is Lothario in ye fair Penitent . . . his Rl Highness would not be said nay.'[2]

The manager occupied a dominating position in the theatre and controlled virtually all of its affairs. He alone held responsibility for selecting the plays for the repertory, casting them, and employing the actors. Murphy, who was Garrick's biographer, argued that the fate of English drama rested in the hands of the theatre managers: 'The public taste, the honour of old English authors, and the state of dramatic poetry in general, are all committed to his care.'[3] However, the evidence available suggests that few theatre managers of the period commanded an ability adequate to fulfill those responsibilities. John Rich, who managed Covent Garden in the years 1732–61, promoted pantomime and showed little sympathy with either actors or new plays. Murphy attacked him as a debaucher of the public taste,[4] but despite these strictures the entertainments which Rich presented proved highly popular with contemporary theatre audiences. Pantomime brought financial success, and eventually Garrick competed with him in such entertainment. G. M. Kahrl pointed out that Garrick 'exploited, at times cynically, the appetite for spectacle, dance, music, farce, and pantomime in the afterpieces . . . the eight most frequently acted pieces during Garrick's management were not plays but pantomimes, farces, one ballad opera, and one so-called "entertainment"'. Moreover, Garrick 'wrote three of the most popular afterpieces: *Harlequin's Invasion, Lethe,* and *The Jubilee*' (*LG*, I, xlix).

When Rich left Covent Garden in 1761 John Beard succeeded him, but Beard was a singer and he encouraged music in the theatre. The popularity of Italian opera, and its English derivations in the form of ballad and comic opera, influenced the repertory at Covent Garden. Dramatists successfully introduced music into serious drama, although John Genest deplored this development and criticized *The Battle of Hexham* as a 'jumble of Tragedy, Comedy, and Opera', the success of which 'encouraged Colman and others to persist in this despicable species of the drama, in defiance of nature and common sense'.[5] The audience's taste for music became costly to satisfy. R. Crompton Rhodes pointed out that in 1773 Mrs Sheridan refused an offer from Samuel Arnold of £3000 for 'twenty performances in oratorio at the Pantheon, and at Giardini's concerts'.[6] William Cooke wrote:

It is curious to regard the difference of times as it respects the state of music and general state of society. In the year 1728, a first rate singer could obtain thirty shillings per week

. . . whilst a first rate singer in the year 1801 was thought worthy of an arbitration between the two rival Managers, contending who should have her, at the rate of three thousand pounds per season, and a clear benefit! [7]

In contrast to the situation at Covent Garden, Garrick took his duties seriously and he worked conscientiously. Davies attributed 'the more advanced state of the stage'[8] to his wise management. He endeavoured to improve theatrical conditions whenever he could. He altered the form of lighting used at Drury Lane so as to reduce the discomfort which the old system imposed upon the eyes of the audience, and in 1765 he abandoned all rights to occupy seats on the stage. This, Yvonne Ffrench argued, 'was one of the last of the conventions linking aristocratic culture to the players' mode of life', and indicated that in the eighteenth century drama became less directed towards the aristocracy and increasingly towards 'the wealthy, rising, fashionable middle classes'.[9] Garrick remained 'zealous at all times for the honour of the English drama',[10] and he wrote contemptuously of pantomime as that 'holiday Nonsense' (*LG,* II, 912). He scorned the use of spectacular devices in the theatre, and condemned *'Maddox's* rope-dancing upon our stage. I cannot possibly agree to such a prostitution upon any account; and nothing but downright starving would induce me to bring such defilement and abomination into the *house of William Shakespeare.* What a mean, mistaken creature is this Par[tn]er of mine! ' (*LG,* I, 172). Garrick declared that his primary interest was in Shakespearean productions; 'Tis my chief wish, my joy, my only plan,/To lose no drop of that immortal man'.[11] Despite this, however, he often produced adapted versions of Shakespeare's plays; and although he included more of the text of *King Lear* than existed in Tate's version, he nevertheless retained the love relationship between Edgar and Cordelia and the happy ending in which Lear was restored to the throne. Lamb was not the first to object to this. In 1747 Samuel Foote had demanded *'Lear* in the *Original,* Fool and all'. He asked Garrick: 'Why will you do so great an Injury to *Shakespeare,* as to perform Tate's execrable Alteration of him?'. And in 1756 Mrs Frances Brooke expressed her 'great astonishment' and her 'surprize, that Mr Garrick, who professes himself so warm an idolater of this inimitable poet, and who is determined . . . "To lose no drop of this immortal man", should yet prefer the vile adulterated cup of *Tate,* to the pure genuine draught, offered him by the master he avows to serve with such fervency of devotion'.[12]

Garrick controlled the theatre shrewdly. He treated actors with greater justice and understanding than they normally received in this period, but, if crossed, he could be severe, and at times revealed the truth of Johnson's comment that he ruled actors 'with a high hand'.[13] In October 1773 Garrick wrote to Charles Dibdin: 'When I send for you I expect both from good manners & Duty, that you will come to me & know what I have to Say, before you will presume to answer it. — You are *our Composer,* & are not to do what *you* please; but what the *Managers* please' (*LG,* II, 901). He also showed his strength in 1775 in the hard bargain which he drove with Smith in order to punish that actor:

> Smith cannot, with the people the Managers have engag'd, be employ'd at Covent Garden – He has offer'd himself to Me by my Brother in a fit of honour, or Compunction – I still keep aloof, & have written a very spirited & refusing letter to him – this my policy & my Spirit requir'd – but I will not hide a thought from You – I really think we can't do without him, & if so (for Henderson is yet disengag'd) how can I make it worth B[arr]y's while to change his Situation? (*LG,* III, 1001).

Garrick could be a little unscrupulous in striving for success, but he gradually built up a stronger company of actors at Drury Lane than existed at Covent Garden. He had great energy, determination, and ambition, and although egotistical he did have a genuine passion for the state of the theatre. He was not ruled simply by selfish motives. He sincerely wanted to assist in the development of English theatre. His deliberately obstructive attitude towards his principal rival, the theatre at Covent Garden, suggested a major concern with his own supremacy, but his behaviour in this respect can be partially explained by his revulsion at the approach to the theatre shown by Rich and Beard. Both Drury Lane and Covent Garden manifested hostility towards one another.

When Garrick retired in 1776 a great era in theatre history ended. He was succeeded as manager by R. B. Sheridan who had established his theatrical fame as a playright. As Lewis Gibbs suggested, Sheridan devoted more energy to politics than to the management of Drury Lane. He had borrowed money in order to buy the patent of the theatre, and he then used the theatre to finance his political career. For many years Drury Lane probably provided his only consistent source of income, and the financial affairs of the theatre became hopelessly confused. Deeply in debt Sheridan did not always pay the salaries of his actors, and Sarah Siddons left the company for a season in protest. The actor-manager, King, who held responsibility but no power to act, became exasperated and in 1778 he resigned. He set out his grievances in a letter to the press.[14] Sheridan retained absolute control over all decisions. The *English Review* compared Garrick's and Sheridan's handling of Drury Lane in these terms: 'The difference of the internal state of the Theatre, when under the direction of Garrick, compared to what followed in the reign of Sheridan, is astonishing. Precision and watchful assiduity were the characteristics of the former, and all was order. Carelessness, neglect, and dissipation, succeeded, and all was anarchy.'[15] Sheridan did not assume his responsibilities. In 1788 he made John Philip Kemble the director of the theatre, and in a speech delivered in the House of Commons, he referred to the time 'when he knew more of what was going on with respect to the theatres than he did at present, having long since entrusted his interest in them to the management of others.'[16] Kemble claimed that during the time that he had spent at Drury Lane waiting for Sheridan he had read more of the manuscripts of new plays submitted for production than Sheridan had read himself. Coleridge lost patience with the endless delays over the decision of Sheridan concerning *Osorio* and he denounced him as an 'unprincipled rogue'.[17]

In 1791 Drury Lane had to be pulled down and Sheridan replaced it with a much larger building. Henry Holland designed the new theatre which seated over two thousand five hundred spectators,[18] but its inadequacies were evident. Hazlitt suggested that the noise from the 'gods' at Drury Lane stemmed primarily from the audience's 'impatience at not being able to hear what is passing below',[19] for at the smaller theatres like the Haymarket this part of the audience were attentive. The new vast theatres ill suited the most skilful actors. Hazlitt's comments on Kean stressed the vital importance of detail of expression as a contribution to the actor's total performance, but a spectator at a great distance in a large theatre could not appreciate this aspect of the actor's technique.

The accompaniment of expression is absolutely necessary to explain his tones and gestures: and the outline which he gives of the character, in proportion as it is bold and decided, requires to be filled up and modified by all the details of execution. Without seeing the workings of his face, through which you read the movements of his soul, and anticipate their violent effects on his utterance and action, it is impossible to understand or feel pleasure in the part. All strong expression, deprived of its gradations and connecting motives, unavoidably degenerates into caricature. (V, 284–5).

Spectacular effects increasingly replaced the subtleties of acting. John Philip Kemble, as stage-manager of Drury Lane, exploited the audience's predilection for spectacle by his extreme concern for historical accuracy of costume and lavish scenery. Sarah Siddons wrote to Lady Harcourt in 1794 that the banquet in *Macbeth* 'is a thing to go and see of itself'.[20] As the public taste for spectacle developed so Kemble resorted to productions like *Bluebeard,* in which animals appeared on the stage; and when Bunn took over the management of the two theatres he completed their debasement to the level of a circus. Shakespearean productions suffered the consequences of this. In 1842 Macready wrote in his Journal: 'After dinner went to Covent Garden and saw the first scene of *The Tempest.* A ship was introduced and all the poetry cut out – worse acting or more inapplicable means to an end I never saw.'[21]

Inevitably there were strong voices of protest. Both Coleridge and Hazlitt lamented the poor state of contemporary theatrical judgement. In a letter to Wordsworth in January 1798, following Sheridan's preference of Matthew Lewis' *Castle Spectre* over *Osorio,* Coleridge wrote:

This Play proves how accurately you conjectured concerning *theatric* merit. The merit of the Castle Spectre consists wholly in it's *situations.* These are all borrowed, and all absolutely *pantomimical;* but they are admirably managed for stage effect . . . This play struck me with utter hopelessness – it would be [easy] to produce these situations, but not in a play so for[cibly] as to admit the permanent & closest beauties of style, passion & character. To admit pantomimic tricks the plot itself must be pantomimic.[22]

Hazlitt accused the managers of resorting to 'every kind of quackery' as if they were 'determined to fill their pockets for the present, and disgust the public in the end, if the public were an animal capable of being disgusted by quackery' (V, 302). He had as little respect for the audiences who enjoyed and demanded these spectacles as for the managers who produced them. In his review of a particularly bad performance of *Richard III* he argued that London's theatre managers seemed 'completely ignorant of their profession' (V, 247).

In addition to the London managers there were others in the provinces. The worst of these controlled poor companies of strolling actors who performed in barns or any available building. They were invariably treated with contempt, and Garrick thought that their acting was abysmal. He wrote to James Love in March 1765: 'I dread a Stroler, they contract such insufferable Affectation that they disgust me – I never could account for the Country Actors being so very wide of ye mark' (*LG*, II, 446). Their productions depended upon their ingenuity in overcoming all kinds of unforeseen problems and were rarely of a good standard. The manager had absolute command over the company, and Holcroft, who had been a stroller himself, explained, in his memoirs, how the company was organized. They preserved some of the Elizabethan traditions, including the system of profit-sharing.[23] However, some groups of strollers acted well. Roger Kemble, the father of Sarah Siddons and John Philip Kemble, managed one such group in the West Midlands, and his journal for 1766–8 recorded an extensive repertory and a period of financial success.[24] Provincial actors could sometimes act on regular circuits and in good theatres. Tate Wilkinson organized a Yorkshire circuit which included actors like Sarah Siddons, John Philip Kemble, and Mrs Jordan before they made their reputations in London. The good provincial theatres provided London with many talented actors, and they formed an important part of the theatrical activity of the period. Towards the end of the eighteenth and the beginning of the nineteenth centuries their numbers increased greatly, and their value was acknowledged by the granting of royal patents. Bath received a patent in 1767, Liverpool in 1770, and Bristol in 1778.

ii

Both Drury Lane and Covent Garden established stable acting companies, and as a result new actors created attention. Lynch pointed out how playbills often used an actor's first appearance to stimulate interest. The actors held tenaciously to principles of seniority and the 'possession of parts' whereby some roles belonged exclusively to various leading actors and could not be acted by any other member of the company. Doran, the nineteenth-century theatre historian, claimed that the possession of parts by the actors King and Smith hindered the early development of John Philip Kemble's career. This practice must have discouraged many young actors.[25]

More significantly, star actors strove with great energy to protect their supremacy, and an element of competition dictated their stage manoeuvres. Kean deliberately sought to overshadow fellow actors like Macready and he acted Booth off the stage. Hazlitt described the tragic actors of Drury Lane as 'supernumeraries' (XVIII, 355) whilst Kean acted there. Drury Lane produced no tragic actors of any eminence during the period in which Kean established himself as the leading tragedian whereas several tragic actors emerged at Covent Garden.[26] Although Macready adopted a deeply serious attitude towards his acting, Archer accurately underlined that his 'artistic scrupulousness . . . was accompanied by a large amount of the inartistic unscrupulousness of the typical "star". His own part was everything; the opportunities of his fellow-actors, and even the poet's text, must all give place to the complete development of his effects'.[27] Talfourd wrote *Glencoe* and *The Athenian Captive* solely for Macready, not for a company of actors, and this tendency had a deleterious effect on the drama. Lesser actors were merely required to play their parts in conventional stereotyped fashion and not distract attention from the 'star'. Peake complained of the problems which this 'star-system' presented to the dramatists.

Alas! times are sadly changed for authors; but in those days there were no ruinous salaries, nor was the star-system in vogue (the stepping-stone to the downfall of the drama of England) . . . At that period, an author could write for a com-

26

pany, but now it must be for an individual; and the individual is paid such a monstrous sum for his nightly performance that the manager is incapacitated from giving a proper remuneration to the author.[28]

Since the actors demanded an opportunity to play their preferred roles, many stock plays were retained in the repertory, and this practice limited the number of new plays which could be produced.

Actors did not work consistently for the benefit of the theatre. They feigned illness, quarrelled through jealousy or pride, and simply refused roles which displeased them. Serious rehearsal rarely took place, and in his preface to *The Iron Chest* Colman the Younger attacked the way in which his play had been prepared for production, because 'there never was one fair rehearsal of the play – never one rehearsal, wherein one, two, or more of the performers, very essential to the piece, were not absent; and all the rehearsals which I attended, so slovenly and irregular'.[29] Garrick's management suffered from the whims and tantrums of his actors and actresses, and he gradually became more easily and more deeply exasperated by the irritating idiosyncrasies of his employees. In January 1776 he expressed a sense of relief that his retirement would at least free him from these vexations:

Mrs. Garrick & I are happy wth the thoughts of my *Strutting & fretting no more upon ye Stage,* & leaving to Younger Spirits the present race of Theatrical Heroines with all their Airs, indispositions, tricks & importances which have reduc'd the Stage to be a dependant upon the Wills of our insolent, vain, & let me add insignificant female trumpery – there must be a revolution, or my Successors will Suffer much, I had a resource in my own Acting, that counteracted all the Evil designs of these Gentry. (*LG,* III, 1063).

Many players placed their individual advantages before those of the theatre. During Sheridan's managership Mrs Jordan refused to act with Mrs Siddons in a farce because, as the press reported, '*she* will not fill the house and let Mrs Siddons run away with the reputation of it'.[30] The actors competed against one another and rarely worked as a team. The theatre lacked discipline.

Not all actors behaved irresponsibly. Many dedicated themselves to their profession, although two of the best examples, Garrick in the eighteenth and Macready in the nineteenth centuries, were not only actors but also managers. They both demonstrated their devotion to the theatre. They realized the necessity for a more disciplined approach from the actors. In letters to William Powell in December 1764 and to John Henderson in January 1773 Garrick stressed the importance of seriousness. He recommended to Powell that 'Study, and an Accurate consideration of Your Characters' demanded many hours, and he added: 'never let your *Shakespear* be out of your hands, or your Pocket' (*LG,* II, 436). In the nineteenth century Macready wrote in his Journal on 28 July 1833:

> I have begun more seriously this month to apply to the study of my profession, impelled by the necessity which the present state of the drama creates. I do not feel that I have the talent to recall attention to an art from which amusement cannot be drawn but by an exertion of the intellect. The age is too indolent in part, and in part too highly cultivated. But while I see the desperate condition to which, at this late period of my life, my profession is reduced, I am not thereby inclined to let my spirits sink under the disheartening prospect. To do my best is still my duty to myself and to my children, and I *will do it.*[31]

They raised standards in their acting companies and increased the good reputation of their profession.

Garrick advised Powell to maintain his integrity and not allow others to encourage him to lower his standards: 'Guard against *the Splitting the Ears of the Groundlings who are Capable of Nothing but dumb Shew, & noise,* – don't sacrifice your taste and ffeelings to the Applause of Multitude; a true Genius will convert an Audience to His Manner, rather than be converted by them to what is false and unnatural' (*LG,* II, 436). To Garrick the 'blackest of all Sins against Nature' was *'Affectation'* (*LG,* II, 442). Garrick, as well as Macklin, encouraged a style of acting which was more natural and realistic than that which had previously existed. In November 1762 Garrick commented on the difference between strolling and London actors and in so doing pointed also to the difference between past and present London actors: 'I don't know how it is, but the Strollers are a hundred years behind hand – We in Town are Endeavouring to bring the Sock & Buskin down to Nature, but *they* still keep to their Strutting, bouncing & mouthing' (*LG,* I, 367). Garrick and

Macklin abandoned formality. Garrick wrote in March 1748 that he had 'been often accus'd of neglecting the Harmony of the Versification, from a too close Regard to the Passion, and the Meaning of the Author' (*LG*, I, 92). Macklin's early attempts to introduce more natural acting in tragedy met with a chill reception: 'I spoke so familiar, Sir, and so little in the hoity-toity tone of the tragedy of that day, that the manager Rich told me I had better go to grass for another year or two.'[32] In 1804 Cooke described the alterations introduced by Macklin and Garrick as 'changing an elevated tone of voice, a mechanical depression of its tones, and a formal measured step in traversing the stage, into an easy familiar manner of speaking and acting'.[33] Action superseded declamation. They also rejected the conventional interpretations of characters which one generation passed on to the next. They asserted the actor's right to re-interpret a role. Garrick's Richard the Third and Macklin's Shylock, both first performed in 1741, offered revolutionary interpretations and met with such outstanding success that they not only assured the reputations of the two actors but also their style of acting.

Towards the end of the eighteenth century John Philip Kemble and Sarah Siddons re-established the strength of a so-called 'classical' style of acting. Hazlitt declared that Kemble was 'the most classical of actors. He is the only one of the moderns, who both in figure and action approaches the beauty and grandeur of the antique' (V, 342). If he could not convey the 'perpetual undulation of feeling' in Hamlet because he was 'too deliberate and formal' (XVIII, 199), yet he commanded attention and acted with an imposing dignity. More recently Whitley argued that 'the classical actor' like Kemble sought 'to rise above nature, to grasp something of the ideal. He is not only portraying the terrible and pathetic fall of one great man; he is at the same time striving after some more abstract quality, the soul of tragedy.'[34] To contemporary audiences this often gave an impression of artificiality. Leigh Hunt found him 'too artificial, too formal, too critically and deliberately conscious'. Sarah Siddons for the most part avoided such criticism and maintained a greater semblance of spontaneity and vitality in her performances, but when Edmund Kean arrived he shattered the tradition of 'classical' acting. Leigh Hunt wrote that 'Kemble faded before him, like a tragedy ghost'.[35] Hazlitt praised Kean's 'bursts of feeling and energy' (V,

189), which contrasted sharply with the techniques of Siddons and Kemble. Coleridge said that to see Kean act was 'like reading Shakespeare by flashes of lightning',[36] but this implied that he performed with only a sporadic brilliance. If Kean sometimes achieved moments of superb insight which captivated the audience, he could at other times act poorly. At his best no-one could match him, but he was inconsistent.

The age also had excellent comic actors and pantomimists. Lamb, Leigh Hunt, and Hazlitt all attempted to recreate the effect of the incomparable antics of men like Munden, Liston, Dodd, and Grimaldi – one of the great clowns of English pantomime. Comic actors received less respect and lower salaries than tragic actors, and social distinctions existed between them. Clowns and harlequins were excluded from the charity of the Royal Theatrical Fund.

The incomes of actors could be supplemented by benefit nights in the last weeks of the season and by provincial tours in the Summer. These tours proved highly lucrative for the 'star' actors who received huge payments, but reinforced the very subordinate position of the supporting actors, so that good all round casting of plays diminished. Macready complained bitterly of the standards of those with whom he was expected to act in the provinces because he considered their incompetence a hindrance to his own performance,[37] but by adhering to the 'star-system' he only perpetuated that situation.

iii

The theatre audiences forcefully illustrated the truth of Johnson's statement that 'The drama's laws the drama's patrons give,/For we that live to please, must please to live.[38] They often behaved violently and sometimes rioted in order to express their feelings and impose their demands on the manager. In November 1744, when Fleetwood raised the admission charges for the evenings on which pantomimes and entertainments were performed, the audience protested and considerably damaged Drury Lane theatre. Other riots occurred at regular intervals.[39] In 1809 John

Philip Kemble faced the 'Old Prices' riots when he too sought to increase admission charges. Both Fleetwood and Kemble were forced to make concessions. The audiences also obliged the actors to respect them. In 1775 Mrs Yates failed to speak an epilogue, and an apology appeared in the *London Chronicle* of 4–7 March 1775, but before Mrs Yates next performed the audience required that she step forward and personally assure them that she had been genuinely unable to speak the epilogue on her previous appearance.

The inattention and unruliness of some parts of the audiences provoked numerous complaints throughout the eighteenth and early nineteenth centuries. Colman the Younger criticized the fashion 'for the bucks and blades, and bloods of the town, to go to a new play on purpose to condemn it; this tumultuous attempt to annihilate anything, and everything, before it could be ascertained to be right or wrong, being denominated good sport, and high fun'.[40] This premeditated hostility to a play stirred authors and managers to counter such disturbances. They sought to fill the theatre with friends, or with persons who were paid to mechanically applaud at various moments in the play. The press also accepted payments from the theatres for the publication of favourable reviews, which were known as 'puffs'. In his autobiography Leigh Hunt wrote of the situation at the very beginning of the nineteenth century:

> Puffing and plenty of tickets were, however, the system of the day. It was an interchange of amenities over the dinner-table; a flattery of power on the one side, and puns on the other; and what the public took for a criticism on a play was a draft upon the box-office, or reminiscences of last Thursday's salmon and lobster-sauce.[41]

Leigh Hunt reacted against this tradition. In the *News,* a paper set up by his brother John in 1805, Leigh Hunt achieved independence in the theatrical criticism which he contributed.

Throughout this period the dramatists could not exceed the rigid restrictions of the audience's moral standards, and they could not deal with politics without risking extraordinarily sensitive reactions. After the French Revolution Holcroft, who was identified with men like Paine, brought out his plays anonymously.[42] Patriotic British audiences would not otherwise have tolerated them. This situation inevitably sapped the vigour of the drama.

31

Many older Elizabethan, Jacobean, and Restoration plays were adapted before they were considered as fit for representation. Garrick, who was acutely aware of contemporary taste, re-wrote many plays in order to expunge immorality. In a letter to Hoadly in August 1746 he claimed that Beaumont and Fletcher's *Philaster* was 'very indecent & requires great alterations' (*LG*, I, 85). A good impression of audience attitudes can be obtained by studying reactions to *King Lear,* which was performed in Tate's version. The reviewer in *The Public Ledger* wrote: 'What mind is so pleased with melancholy Ideas, or the struggles of injured virtue in distress, as not to receive much heart-felt satisfaction, in the last Scene, where *Edgar* and *Cordelia,* surmounting all difficulties, are made happy in each other's love, as a reward for their loyalty and virtue?'[43] Theatrical reviewers reinforced the audience's predilection for morality. In *The London Daily Advertiser and Literary Gazette* of 4 November 1751 the reviewer wrote: 'We cannot see Qualities like those of *Glouster, Edgar,* and *Cordelia,* become the Sources of Misfortune, without Horror; and are vexed to see Perfidy, Baseness, and Ingratitude, like those of *Edmund* and the two other *Daughters,* represented as Inhabitants of Breasts of the same Species with our own'. He praised Tate for making the 'Catastrophe favourable to his virtuous Characters: Without this the Play could not have borne a second Hearing; but even with this Advantage it hurts us; we are not reconciled to the Rewards, great as they are, when purchased at the Expence of so much unmerited Pain'. If Tate's version generated such ideas then Shakespeare's play clearly had no prospect of performance. Eighteenth-century audiences preferred to see the virtuous rewarded and the wicked punished. They found it difficult to countenance injustice on the stage.

Johnson argued that Cordelia's death was 'contrary to the natural ideas of justice', and he confessed: 'I was many years ago so shocked by Cordelia's death, that I know not whether I ever endured to read again the last scenes of the play till I undertook to revise them as an editor.' He thought that if 'other excellencies are equal' the audience would 'always rise better pleased from the final triumph of persecuted virtue'. He published Shakespeare's text but he insisted that poetry afford moral instruction, and this led him to point out a very important 'defect' in Shakespeare:

He sacrifices virtue to convenience, and is so much more careful to please than to instruct, that he seems to write without any moral purpose. From his writings indeed a system of social duty may be selected, for he that thinks reasonably must think morally; but his precepts and axioms drop casually from him; he makes no just distribution of good or evil, nor is always careful to shew in the virtuous a disapprobation of the wicked; he carries his persons indifferently through right and wrong, and at the close dismisses them without further care, and leaves their examples to operate by chance. This fault the barbarity of his age cannot extenuate; for it is always a writer's duty to make the world better, and justice is a virtue independant on time or place.[44]

In this instance Johnson's views supported the prevailing demands of contemporary theatre audiences.

iv

The eighteenth century produced increasing numbers of sentimental comedies, pathetic tragedies, and comic operas, despite the challenge from Sheridan and Goldsmith who sought to inject some vitality into comedy. A situation developed whereby dramatists like Frederick Reynolds obtained their most lucrative rewards from afterpieces and short musicals, and these, Reynolds declared, were the easiest plays to write.[45] Fewer five act comedies appeared, and melodrama became dominant in the theatre. Theatrical conditions cramped the development of new dramatists, and Goldsmith rightly lamented a situation in which the theatre became the independent commerce of an individual,[46] since it meant that no manager felt he could risk his livelihood to finance apprentice dramatists. No room existed for serious experiment. Moreover, many men of letters had received formal educations and laboured under neo-classical critical theory. When Goldsmith reviewed Home's *Douglas* in *The Monthly Review,* he argued that a 'mechanically exact adherence to all the rules of the Drama, is more the business of industry than of genius'.[47] He suggested that too many dramatists adhered too literally to critical precepts, and that they failed to exercise an independent taste or judgement.

Very many of the new plays performed were written by established managers and actors whose thorough knowledge of the theatre enabled them to suit their plays to the prevailing theatrical conditions more easily than those writers who lacked experience of the theatre. Moreover, managers and actors occupied influential positions which undoubtedly increased their possibilities of staging their plays. Since managers alone decided which plays to perform or reject they became subject to some reasonable as well as some scurrilous criticism. They were attacked for their alleged 'avarice and self-interest' and because they 'suppressed many an excellent performance, to make room for their own pieces'.[48] Such extravagant claims for the quality of the plays which did not reach the stage cannot be substantiated.

Since writers without connections in the theatre found it difficult to convince managers to produce their plays, they sometimes solicited influential public figures to exert pressure on the manager. Garrick wrote of the dilemma which such a situation could provoke:

> I have a Play now with Me, sent to Me by My Lord Chesterfield & wrote by One Smollet; it is a Scotch Story, but it won't do, & yet recommended by his Lordship & patroniz'd by Ladies of Quality: what can I say, or do? must I belye my Judgment or run the risque of being thought impertinent, & disobliging ye Great Folks? (*LG,* I, 86).

These discouragements turned writers like Smollett to exercise their talents in other literary genres. Goldsmith, in his *An Enquiry into the Present State of Polite Learning in Europe,* published in 1759, argued that 'getting a play on even in three or four years, is a privilege reserved only for the happy few who have the arts of courting the manager as well as the muse', and he warned of the dangers which this involved: 'For the future, it is somewhat unlikely, that he, whose labours are valuable, or who knows their value, will turn to the stage for either fame or subsistence.'[49]

In their anxiety to obtain performances of their plays even the best authors adopted the most humiliating positions. Goldsmith pleaded his poverty to Colman and proposed that 'whatever objections you have made, or shall make, to my play, I will endeavour to remove, and not argue about them'.[50] However, the theatre seasons were organized in such a way that with all of the stock plays which the actors demanded, and the numerous end of season 'benefit' nights, little time remained for the production of new plays. In September 1774 Garrick wrote to Sir Joshua Reynolds: 'I have no less than Seven Plays, Each of 5 acts, & two smaller pieces for representation; these with our reviv'd Plays will be as much as any Manager can thrust with all his might into two Seasons' (*LG,* III, 955). Thus it seems that only three or four new 5 act plays could be presented in one season.

Dramatists occupied a subordinate position in the theatre and could neither command the attention nor exert the influence which actors enjoyed. If an actor demanded an alteration in a play his wish was usually satisfied. But the dramatists did derive great benefit from the high quality of many of the actors. In 1807 Leigh Hunt wrote that 'at the comedies of Mr REYNOLDS and of Mr DIBDIN, . . . I laughed very heartily at the grimaces of the actors; but somehow or another I never recollected a word of the dialogue'. Authors increasingly relied upon the actors, and Hunt added that the loss of Lewis would be as rheumatism to Reynolds, and the loss of Munden, 'who gives such agreeable variety of grin, would affect him little less than lock-jaw'.[51] Naturally, actors could also ruin a play's prospects if they so decided, and Colman the Younger maintained that John Philip Kemble deliberately prevented the success of his play *The Iron Chest.* Moreover, three hours before the first performance the theatre obliged Colman to agree to 'a transposition of two of the most material scenes in the second act'[52] because the scenery could not be changed quickly enough. Authors were often treated with scant respect.

One of the most outstanding plays of the period was Shelley's *The Cenci.* On a number of occasions Shelley expressed an intense dislike for the theatre, as did Byron, who in the well-known preface to *Marino Faliero* explained his abhorrence at submitting his work to

> the mercies of an audience: – the sneering reader, and the loud critic, and the tart review, are scattered and distant calamities; but the trampling of an intelligent or of an ignorant audience on a production which, be it good or bad, has been a mental labour to the writer, is a palpable and immediate

grievance, heightened by a man's doubt of their competency to judge, and his certainty of his own imprudence in electing them his judges.[53]

Years of vain attempts at theatrical success had now convinced some authors that writing for the theatre did not warrant the trouble which it involved – precisely the situation foreseen by Goldsmith. But this did not apply to Shelley's *The Cenci.* He wrote with the theatre in his mind and sent the play to Harris, who was manager of Covent Garden; but Harris rejected it because he found 'the subject to be so objectionable that he could not even submit the part to Miss O'Neil for perusal'.[54] Shelley had written the play with this very anxiety in mind: 'my principal doubt as to whether it would succeed as an acting play hangs entirely on the question as to whether any such a thing as incest in this shape, however treated, would be admitted on the stage.'[55] He clearly hoped to have his play performed but contemporary prudishness rendered those hopes futile. If he had not yet thoroughly mastered the art of writing for the theatre he nevertheless displayed rare skills. Perhaps he had the ability to develop into a major dramatist, but the nineteenth century refused him that opportunity.

II Lamb as Critic of Dramatic Literature

The *Specimens of English Dramatic Poets* and *Extracts from the Garrick Plays* illustrate a number of fundamental ideas which governed Lamb's criticism, and they afford an insight into his excellence as a critic of dramatic literature, particularly in his comments on the subjectivity of the creative process and on decorum as an aesthetic as well as ethical standard for the evaluation of art. In the *Specimens* and *Extracts* Lamb was not a critic of the theatre, in the strict sense, for he never witnessed stage performance of these plays, and his critical notes consequently paid only the slightest attention to the theatrical qualities of the extracts chosen. F. V. Morley argued that Lamb 'encouraged a nineteenth-century distinction between plays as poetry and plays as drama',[1] but the circumstances which surrounded publication of the *Specimens* and *Extracts* forced this distinction. Lamb's critical responses differed according to the artistic medium by which a work was presented to him, as he made clear in the essay on Shakespearean tragedy. He did not create an artificial approach to drama by appreciating it as poetry, but rather realised that the critical perspective which accompanied theatrical experience could not be removed to another context, such as the study, and remain meaningful. To read a play in the study was to perform an act of literary and not theatrical criticism.

Lamb's preface to the first edition of the *Specimens,* which he published in 1808, commands close attention because it clarifies our understanding of his initial conception of his work. He did not, at that time, regard pioneering on behalf of Elizabethan and Jacobean dramatists as his primary purpose, although many commentators have stressed only this aspect of his work. When James Shokhoff recently referred to Lamb's 'objectives' the quotations which he selected did not fully reflect the balance between Lamb's critical and historical importance: 'Lamb's objectives are to call attention to "what we have slighted, while beyond all proportion we have cried up one or two favourite names," and to show "how much of Shakespeare shines in the great men his contemporaries, and how far in his divine mind and manners he surpassed them and all mankind.'"[2] Lamb stated that 'his leading design' was 'to illustrate what may be called the moral sense of our ancestors' (IV, xii). This necessitated criticism. In the selection and evaluation of appropriate material, and in the notes which he wrote, Lamb acted as literary critic and not merely as one documenting the drama of the past. He sought plays 'which treat of human life and manners, rather than masques, and Arcadian pastorals, with their train of abstractions, unimpassioned deities, passionate mortals, Claius, and Medorus, and Amintas, and Amarillis' (IV, xi-xii). Just as he attacked abstraction in the poetry of Coleridge and Byron so here he rejected it again.

He himself drew attention to the historical value of the work when in an autobiographical sketch in 1827 he declared himself 'the first to draw the Public attention to the old English Dramatists in a work called "Specimens of English Dramatic Writers who lived about the time of Shakespeare"' (I, 321). Critics have failed to agree on the seriousness as well as the accuracy of this remark. D. S. Perry argued that it was only a 'careless off-hand statement in the mood of the whole little sketch'.[3] But Lamb had reacted with genuine exasperation to the way in which his contemporaries looked upon these dramatists, and probably believed that a book like his *Specimens* fulfilled a serious and important role. He had complained to Coleridge in June 1796:

> I wish you would try and do something to bring our elder bards into more general fame. I writhe with indignation when in books of Criticism, where common place quotation is heaped upon quotation, I find no mention of such men as Massinger, or B. and Fl, men with whom succeeding Dramatic Writers (Otway alone excepted) can bear no manner of comparison. Stupid Knox hath noticed none of 'em among his extracts. (*Letters,* I, 32).

In Lamb's opinion, the contemporary critical evaluation underestimated the Elizabethan and Jacobean dramatists, and he charged Coleridge to change this. Coleridge was the man whom Lamb, especially at this period of his life, most esteemed, and he would not have asked him to consider a task which he did not think worthy of his friend's genius. But eventually he did the work himself, and at the time of publication he wrote a letter to Manning on 26 February 1808 in which he did not disguise his pleasure: 'the book is such as I am glad there should be. It is done out of old plays at the Museum and out of Dodsley's collection, &c. It is to have notes' (*Letters*, II, 49). Lamb took a pride in his achievement.

His claim to originate attention stressed the *Public* nature of his work, with an implicit contrast with the scholarly work of others. He did not delude himself about originality. He knew that he followed previous editors and that he reprinted some material which was already available; but he also realised that many of the extracts which he included had long been forgotten and out of print. He acknowledged in his preface that he borrowed from 'Dodsley's and Hawkins's collections, and the works of Jonson, Beaumont and Fletcher, and Massinger' (IV, xi), but, as Shokhoff pointed out, several plays received their first printing since the seventeenth century, including Ford's *The Lover's Melancholy, The Ladies Trial, Love's Sacrifice,* and *Perkin Warbeck*.[4] During the 1930s the research of Wassermann and Williams placed Lamb in a wider context of developing attention to Elizabethan and Jacobean drama. Williams rightly concluded that the work of Lamb and of the scholars was 'complementary. The editors contributed to the knowledge, Lamb to the more popular appreciation of the Elizabethan and Jacobean drama. But Lamb made use of the texts and notes of the editors who had preceded him, and added his appreciations, which undoubtedly stimulated the endeavours of the editors who followed him'.[5] More recently Shokhoff acknowledged the truth of the strictures of Williams, and provided a fine summary of Lamb's contribution to the Elizabethan revival. He argued that

The Elizabethan revival before Lamb slighted the minor dramatists; that Lamb's *Specimens* was different and more likely to be effective than any other book in the antiquarian movement; that Lamb as scholar-editor was directly responsible for recovering several virtually lost works; and that Lamb's work was a major impetus for and influence upon important studies of the Elizabethan drama after 1808.[6]

The *Specimens* was undoubtedly an influential work. It stimulated Hazlitt's lectures on the Elizabethan and Jacobean dramatists, and in his published text Hazlitt repeated many of Lamb's critical judgements. Moreover, later editors like Barron Field, R. H. Shepherd, John Churton Collins, A. H. Bullen, and Alexander

Dyce acknowledged Lamb's seminal work, and his comments frequently provided convenient quotations for them to incorporate into their own notes and introductions.[7]

If Swinburne inadvisedly attributed Lamb with sole credit for the Elizabethan revival, Klingopulos equally unwisely sneered at him as a propagandist.[8] Some of the ideas included in the notes to the *Specimens* and *Extracts* exerted an influence throughout his criticism of both literature and painting. The comment on Beaumont and Fletcher's *The Maid's Tragedy* revealed his thoughts on the subjectivity of the creative process and on the necessity of decorum in art. For Lamb decorum could refer to aesthetic quality, as indeed it could for Hazlitt who argued that 'Poetry and the stage do not agree together. The attempt to reconcile them fails not only of effect but of decorum' (V, 234). Lamb compared Aspatia in *The Maid's Tragedy* with Zelmane in Sidney's *Arcadia* and with Helena in *Alls Well That Ends Well*, because each author could 'bestow grace upon subjects which naturally do not seem susceptible of any'. This ability depended upon the artist's mind and 'true poetry and passion' which could 'confer dignity upon subjects which do not seem capable of it'. Thus the particular characteristics of Sidney's mind prevented him from articulating indecorous thought and enabled him to preserve a 'matchless decorum'. 'In the sweetly constituted mind of Sir Philip Sidney it seems as if no ugly thought nor unhandsome meditation could find a harbour. He turned all that he touched into images of honour and virtue' (IV, 285). Sidney's work reflected the qualities of his own consciousness. Lamb also applied this idea in critical comments on Shakespeare, Wordsworth, and Hogarth. In a letter to Robert Lloyd on 26 June 1801 he argued that Shakespeare's humanity tempered the evil of Richard the Third, because Shakespeare 'set out to paint a *monster*, but his human sympathies produced a *man*' (Letters, I, 260). In the *Extracts* Lamb commented upon Davenport's *King John and Matilda:*

That the venomous John could have even counterfeited repentance so well, is out of nature; but, supposing the possibility, nothing is truer than the way in which it is managed. These old play-wrights invested their bad characters with notions of good, which could by no possibility have coexisted with their actions. Without a soul of goodness in himself, how could Shakspeare's Richard the Third have lit upon those sweet phrases and inducements by which he attempts to win over the dowager queen to let him wed her daughter? It is not Nature's nature, but Imagination's substituted nature, which does almost as well in a fiction. (IV, 401).

He also suggested that the presentation of nature in Wordsworth's *The Excursion* depended upon the poet's own imagination:

To a mind constituted like that of Mr Wordsworth, the stream, the torrent, and the stirring leaf – seem not merely to suggest associations of deity, but to be a kind of speaking communication with it. He walks through every forest, as through some Dodona; and every bird that flits among the leaves, like that miraculous one in Tasso, but in language more intelligent, reveals to him far higher love-lays. (I, 163).

Similarly Hogarth, who seemed to Lamb to have a mind 'eminently reflective', revealed this quality in the presentation of his characters: 'They have intense thinking faces, though the purpose to which they are subservient by no means required it; but indeed it seems as if it was painful to Hogarth to contemplate mere vacancy or insignificance' (I, 78).

The perceptive critic's response to the work of these men depended upon the manner in which they presented their subjects as well as on the nature of the material itself. Although Hogarth dealt with ostensibly vulgar subjects, he handled them in such a way that he did not create an impression simply of vulgarity. 'To confound the painting of subjects in common or vulgar life with the being a vulgar artist' (I, 73) appeared to Lamb as equally superficial a judgement as that advanced by those who attacked Wordsworth because they mistook 'poetry "having children for its subject" with poetry that is "childish". (I, 171). Lamb argued that the 'quantity of thought which Hogarth crowds into every picture, would alone *unvulgarize* every subject which he might choose' (I, 73). When artists like Shakespeare and Sidney dealt with a supposedly 'dangerous subject' they consciously manipulated their material and 'artfully contrived' (IV, 285) situations so as to create their desired effect on the readers. Shakespeare treated his Helena with such an 'exquisite address' that 'delicacy dispenses with her laws in her favour, and Nature in her single case seems content to suffer a sweet violation' (IV, 285). In this way he preserved the decorum of his work, and Lamb based his judgement of decorum on the author's presentation of his material rather than on the mere content of the material.

This meant that unlike the majority of his contemporaries he did not find the morality of Webster's *Duchess of Malfi* objectionable. Lesser writers lacked decorum but not Webster:

> To move a horror skilfully, to touch a soul to the quick, to lay upon fear as much as it can bear, to wean and weary a life till it is ready to drop, and then step in with mortal instruments to take its last forfeit – this only a Webster can do. Writers of inferior genius may 'upon horror's head horrors accumulate', but they cannot do this. They mistake quantity for quality, they 'terrify babes with painted devils', but they know not how a soul is capable of being moved; their terrors want dignity, their affrightments are without decorum. (IV, 179)

This comment presented decorum as an aesthetic quality. In his essay on the 'Barrenness of the Imaginative Faculty in the Productions of Modern Art' Lamb again used the term decorum to include a reference to the artist's aesthetic values, when he commented upon Raphael's picture of the 'Presentation of the New-born Eve to Adam the Almighty'. He stressed the decorum of the artist's conception: 'The *moment* is seized by the intuitive artist, perhaps not self-conscious of his art, in which neither of the conflicting emotions – a moment how abstracted – have had time to spring up, or to battle for indecorous mastery' (II, 227). Intuition guided the artist and the decorum depended upon judgement. Moreover, this concept of the central role of the intuition in decorum linked decorum to Lamb's belief in the subjectivity of the creative process in which he thought that the artist trusted his intuitive responses.

In his essay 'On the Tragedies of Shakspeare' Lamb commented upon the lack of decorum in Nahum Tate's version of *King Lear*. He objected to the happy ending which Tate had introduced, 'as if the living martyrdom that Lear had gone through, – the flaying of his feelings alive, did not make a fair dismissal from the stage of life the only decorous thing for him' (I, 107). Tate's ending of the play bore no relation to the earlier developments presented in it. His inadequate perception had failed to appreciate the essential elements of Lear's character and situation, and he did not realize that in the light of the whole play Shakespeare's conclusion was both prepared for and necessary. The ending of Tate's version did not harmonise with the rest of the play, and so it lacked decorum. If the different parts of a work did not blend together then Lamb regarded that as artistic weakness. He believed that one of Chapman's limitations was inadequate discrimination: 'He pours out in the same breath the most just and natural and the most violent and forced expressions. He seems to grasp whatever words come first to hand during the impetus of inspiration' (IV, 83). He lacked that judgement which enabled a writer like Shakespeare to know 'to what pitch a passion is becoming; to give the reins and pull in the curb exactly at the moment when the drawing in or the slackening is most graceful' (I, 98). The terms 'becoming' and 'graceful' were linked to Shakespeare's decorum. Chapman lacked a balance of feeling and reason. As Hazlitt argued, the two qualities were complementary: 'Both are imperfect, both are useful in their own ways, and therefore both are best together, to correct or to confirm one another' (VIII, 35).

The absence of artistic judgement which betrayed a lack of decorum could also betray an 'imperfect moral sensibility'. In his comment on Fletcher's *Thierry and Theoderet* Lamb complained of 'unnatural and violent situations' and added that 'Shakspeare had nothing of this contortion in his mind, none of that craving after romantic incidents, and flights of strained and improbable virtue, which I think always betrays an imperfect moral sensibility' (IV, 329). Both decorum and moral sense involved an artist's aesthetic judgement and were not exclusively ethical qualities.

When Lamb announced his decision to illustrate the moral sense of the Elizabethan and Jacobean dramatists, he understood his task to consist in demonstrating 'in what manner they felt, when they placed themselves by the power of imagination in trying situations, in the conflicts of duty and passion, or the strife of contending duties; what sort of loves and enmities theirs were; how their griefs were tempered, and their full-swoln joys abated' (IV, xii). His interest centred upon a critical inquiry into the presentation which distinguished these dramatists; and in the development of this inquiry and the clarification of his judgements, he frequently commented upon the dramatists of his own age, so that he became a critic of contemporary as well as older drama, but with a fundamental difference of approach in that he commented upon contemporary drama as theatre and upon the older drama as literature. Thus, his comments upon Middleton and Rowley's *A Fair Quarrel,* and upon Rowley's *A New Wonder; a Woman Vext,* not only elucidated his understanding of the moral sense of the Elizabethans and Jacobeans, but also highlighted the differences which existed between them and his contemporaries:

> To know the boundaries of honour, to be judiciously valiant, to have a temperance which shall beget a smoothness in the angry swellings of youth, to esteem life as nothing when the sacred reputation of a parent is to be defended, yet to shake and tremble under a pious cowardice when that ark of an honest confidence is found to be frail and tottering, to feel the true blows of a real disgrace blunting that sword which the imaginary strokes of a supposed false imputation had put so keen an edge upon but lately; to do, or to imagine this done in a feigned story, asks something more of a moral sense, somewhat a greater delicacy of perception in questions of right and wrong, than goes to the writing of two or three hackneyed sentences about the laws of honour as opposed to the laws of the land, or a common-place against duelling. Yet such things would stand a writer now-a-days in far better stead than Captain Ager and his conscientious honour; and he would be considered as a far better teacher of morality than old Rowley or Middleton, if they were living. (IV, 115).

A moral sense unaccompanied by powers of discernment produced facile responses. The Elizabethan and Jacobean dramatists possessed a moral sense which enabled them to perceive and understand the complex interaction of the ideas behind moral issues, and which led them to formulate independent judgements. They exercised 'the power of imagination' (IV, xii), and they did not resort, as Lamb claimed that his contemporaries did, to 'a common stock of dramatic morality' (IV, 115) which was slavishly copied and which removed the necessity of original thought. Although he believed that the writers of the Elizabethan and Jacobean periods were part of 'a great race, all of whom spoke nearly the same language, and had a set of moral feelings and notions in common' (IV, 373), he regarded them as significantly distinct from each other. Their independent spirit enabled them to resist the temptation to follow Shakespeare too closely:

'That he was their elder Brother, not their Parent, is evident from the fact of the very few direct imitations of him to be found in their writings. Webster, Decker, Heywood, and the rest of his great contemporaries went on their own ways, and followed their individual impulses, not blindly prescribing to themselves his tract' (IV, 426). No complacency existed in them, whereas Lamb's contemporaries lacked the 'honest boldness' (IV, 126) of those earlier writers and manifested instead a 'hypocritical meekness' (IV, 114).

Lamb accused contemporary dramatists of a lack of originality. He argued that they reduced moral questions to the assumed duties which they entailed, whereas the Elizabethans and Jacobeans 'could discern in the differences, the quarrels, the animosities of man, a beauty and truth of moral feeling, no less than in the iterately inculcated duties of forgiveness and atonement' (IV, 114). Contemporary dramatists did not see below the surface. They 'turn away from the real essences of things to hunt after their relative shadows, moral duties: whereas, if the truth of things were fairly represented, the relative duties might be safely trusted to themselves, and moral philosophy lose the name of a science' (IV, 126). Lamb did not like to be instructed. In a letter to Wordsworth on 30 January 1801 he argued that 'An intelligent reader finds a sort of insult in being told, I will teach you how to think upon this subject'. He disliked authors who 'continually put a sign post up to shew where you are to feel' (*Letters,* I, 239). He objected to an obtrusive didacticism. In his note on Dekker's *The Honest Whore* he suggested that Bellafront's 'simple picture of Honour and Shame, contrasted without violence, and expressed without immodesty, is worth all the *strong lines* against the Harlot's Profession, with which both Parts of this play are offensively crowded' (IV, 55).

Lamb did not believe the function of art to be primarily didactic, and in a letter to Coleridge in 1796 he criticized editors like Vicesimus Knox, who declared in the introduction to his book of *Elegant Extracts* that 'Poetry, by the gentle yet certain method of allurement, leads both to learning and to virtue'.[9] Lamb approached his task in the *Specimens* and the *Extracts from the Garrick Plays* with an emphatically different attitude. Perspectives like those of Knox contributed to the development of a situation which Lamb deplored: 'The insipid levelling morality to which the modern stage is tied down would not admit of such admirable passions as these scenes are filled with. A puritanical obtuseness of sentiment, a stupid infantile goodness, is creeping among us, instead of the vigorous passions, and virtues clad in flesh and blood, with which the old dramatists present us' (IV, 114). He detected in his period a 'Decay of Symbols . . . which whether it has contributed or not to make us a more intellectual, has certainly made us a less imaginative people. Shakspeare knew the force of signs: – "a malignant and a turban'd Turk"' (IV, 71). Wordsworth also argued, in his preface to the *Lyrical Ballads,* that there were forces acting 'to blunt the discriminating powers of the mind' and he stated that 'the literature and theatrical exhibitions of the country have conformed themselves' to the tendencies of the age.[10] Lamb complained that theatre audiences attended performances to 'be complimented upon their goodness' (IV, 114), and to derive 'a certain soothing of self-referred satisfaction' (IV, 126). They applied the virtuous moral values, which they assumed that they possessed in their own characters, to what they saw in the theatre, and thus the conventional moral standards of society exerted a very powerful influence on their theatrical responses. Lamb's arguments implied that they disliked art which challenged the traditional and that they satisfied themselves with superficiality. This also applied to their reading of poetry. In his review of *The Excursion* Lamb wrote:

> The causes which have prevented the poetry of Mr Wordsworth from attaining its full share of popularity are to be found in the boldness and originality of his genius. The times are past when a poet could securely follow the direction of his own mind into whatever tracts it might lead. A writer, who would be popular, must timidly coast the shore of prescribed sentiment and sympathy. He must have just as much more of the imaginative faculty than his readers, as will serve to keep their apprehensions from stagnating, but not so much as to alarm their jealousy. He must not think or feel too deeply. (I, 170).

Contemporary dramatists erred when they accepted the limitations imposed upon their work by their audiences. Lamb's clearly stated opposition to both the dramatists and the audiences provoked contemporary commentators on the *Specimens* to attack his 'disposition to cavil with the taste of the present age, in a tone of much asperity'.[11] He separated himself from the contemporary approach to the theatre because he did not accept the idea that the theatre should be required to reflect the moral standards of its audiences. This principal also influenced his essay 'On the Artificial Comedy of the Last Century'. He considered 'artificial comedy' as entertainment and reproached those who 'dare not contemplate an Atlantis, a scheme, out of which our coxcombical moral sense is for a little transitory ease excluded' (II, 144).

In *The Literary Critics* George Watson argued that the 'moral assumptions' of Lamb's criticism 'are not exactly stern. But they are conventional, a part of that continuum of English prudery that has its roots in eighteenth-century middle-class piety and looks forward to the great Victorian censorship'.[12] Lamb encouraged such judgements when in his preface he announced: 'I have expunged without ceremony all that which the writers had better never have written, that forms the objection so often repeated to the promiscuous reading of Fletcher, Massinger, and some others' (IV, xi). But Lamb's statements did not necessarily acknowledge an agreement with the attitudes which he has nonetheless respected. Some of his comments in the *Specimens* cast doubt on the alleged conventional piety of his criticism. He attacked the moralistic attitude to the theatre displayed by his contemporaries. He reacted favourably to Webster and Marlowe; and in his comment on a scene in Ford's *The Broken Heart* he wrote: 'the expression of this transcendent scene almost bears me in imagination to Calvary and the Cross; and I seem to perceive some analogy between the scenical sufferings which I am here contemplating, and the real agonies of that final completion to which I dare no more than hint a reference' (IV, 218). Gifford regarded this as blasphemy.[13]

The alleged conventional piety of Lamb's criticism cannot be convincingly demonstrated by quotations from the notes to the *Specimens* and *Extracts*. Comments which appear to exhibit pious attitudes often contain implications which cast doubt on Lamb's supposed piety. For example, he commented as follows on Massinger and Dekker's *The Virgin Martyr:*

> This scene has beauties of so very high an order that with all my respect for Massinger, I do not think he had poetical enthusiasm capable of furnishing them. His associate Decker, who wrote Old Fortunatus, had poetry enough for any thing.

47

The very impurities which obtrude themselves among the sweet pieties of this play (like Satan among the Sons of Heaven) and which the brief scope of my plan fortunately enables me to leave out, have a strength of contrast, a raciness, and a glow in them, which are above Massinger. They set off the religion of the rest, somehow as Caliban serves to shew Miranda. (IV, 358).

Before judging a phrase like 'which the brief scope of my plan fortunately enables me to leave out' as pious, Lamb's whole comment needs scrutiny. The phrase rested awkwardly in the context of his total appreciation of the play. Those 'very impurities' seemed to contribute meaningfully to the play, enhancing rather than diminishing its value and interest. The comparison with Caliban and Miranda reinforced the idea that the opposition of the 'impurities' and the 'pieties' improved the play. The 'impurities' heightened awareness and apprehension of the 'religion of the rest'. The terms with which Lamb described the 'impurities' suggested a favourable reaction to them – 'a strength of contrast, a raciness, and a glow' – and in the context of his greater respect for the poetry of Dekker than for that of Massinger, the suggestion that those qualities were 'above' Massinger implied that they were too good to have been written by him. When Lamb regarded it as his good fortune to be able to omit the 'impurities' he did so not because he objected to the inclusion of such material in the play. He respected its value. His good fortune perhaps consisted in the ease with which his plan permitted him to avoid a situation which might have provoked an unfavourable moral reaction against the writers whom he sought to recommend. This showed his awareness of the tastes of his contemporary reading public, but it did not necessarily imply that he shared those tastes.

In his comment on Peele's *The Love of King David and Fair Bethsabe* he wrote: 'There is more of the same stuff, but I suppose the reader has a surfeit; especially as this Canticle of David has never been suspected to contain any pious sense couched underneath it, whatever his son's may' (IV,13). Lamb concealed his own thought here, for the reader's expectations cannot necessarily be assumed to be his also. Again some doubt surrounds the interpretation of Lamb's comment as an expression of conventional piety. He disliked the play and damned it with faint praise, but the comment centred on the word 'Canticle' which by definition would be expected to contain the 'pious sense' which it lacked. The absence of that quality involved the kind of incongruity to which Lamb's criticism frequently objected. It violated decorum and that perhaps provided a valid reason for him to break off the extract. Moreover, in view of his criticism elsewhere in the *Specimens* of the desire of his contemporary audiences for scenes which displayed moral virtue, his comment rather implied that his reader's interest would have waned because of the absence of any 'pious sense'.

Lamb's comment on Fletcher's *The Faithful Shepherdess* also suggested a moral judgement.

If all the parts of this Play had been in unison with these innocent scenes, and sweet lyric intermixtures, it had been a Poem fit to vie with Comus or the Arcadia, to have been put into the hands of boys and virgins, to have made matter for young dreams, like the loves of Hermia and Lysander. But a spot is on the face of this moon. – Nothing short of infatuation could have driven Fletcher upon mixing up with this blessedness such an ugly deformity as Cloe: the wanton shepherdess! Coarse words do but wound the ears; but a character of lewdness affronts the mind. Female lewdness at once shocks nature and morality. If Cloe was meant to set off Clorin by contrast, Fletcher should have known that such weeds by juxtaposition do not set off, but kill sweet flowers. (IV, 312).

Lamb attacked Fletcher's critical judgement for the failure of this play. Fletcher sought to combine diametrically opposed elements in it and produced incongruity. He introduced a character of 'ugly deformity' in a play which contained 'innocent scenes, and sweet lyric intermixtures' and which in 1818 Lamb described as 'delightful pastoral' (I, 55). In the essay 'On the Artificial Comedy of the Last Century' Lamb argued that Congreve omitted pure characters from plays which dealt with libertinous moral attitudes and thus avoided moral judgements (at least in Lamb's case). In Fletcher's play the context in which the 'character of lewdness' appeared partly determined the shocked reaction of a reader. Fletcher lacked decorum. His fault was partly aesthetic.

Perhaps those who emphasize the conventional nature of Lamb's mind do not sufficiently examine the distinction between the views which he held personally and those which he seemed

49

to present to the reading public of the *Specimens*. The bowdleriza-
tion which he admitted in the preface perhaps sought to overcome
the obstacle of the prejudice of his potential readers against the
morality of the Elizabethan and Jacobean dramatists; and this
helped the practical matter of selling the book. His fierce reaction
to Southey's comment on the *Essays of Elia* showed his sensitivity
to the effect which accusations of unconventional views could
have upon a reading public. With reference to Southey's comment Lamb wrote to Bernard Barton on 10 July 1823 that the
'hint he has dropped will knock the sale of the book on the head'
(*Letters*, II, 393). In 1808 Lamb compromised with his reading
public.

The criticism in the *Specimens* and *Extracts* has also been dis-
paraged as impressionist. Wimsatt and Brooks argued that Lamb
as well as Hazlitt shared the 'philosophy of impressionist criticism'
which believed '(1) that the most necessary, or the only necessary
equipment of the critic is his sensibility . . . (2) That, as the artist
himself is the person most susceptible to impressions of beauty,
the artist himself is the only licensed critic . . . (3) That a good
critic, in virtue of his very criticism, is a true artist, or the truest
artist'.[14] The importance which Lamb and Hazlitt attributed to
feeling should not obscure the equal stress which they placed
upon reason. Hazlitt wrote that 'the human mind is a thinking
principle, it is natural to it to think, it cannot feel without thinking' (I, 69). Lamb certainly produced personal impressions in his
criticism, and his judgements reflected the insight of an intuitive
mind, but this formed only a part of his criticism. He was not
simply impressionist when he explored the consequences for
dramatic art of the different relationships which existed between
writers and their publics in the Elizabethan and Jacobean periods
and in the nineteenth century. He was not simply impressionist
when he used Shakespeare as an acknowledged standard against
which to measure literary achievement, and when he commented
on decorum and moral sense as principles for the consideration
of literary works. The notes to the *Specimens* and *Extracts* suggest that impressionism was only one of the modes of critical
thought which he applied in his criticism. He differed from an
impressionist like Oscar Wilde who could argue that 'temperament is the primary requisite for the critic – a temperament
exquisitely susceptible to beauty'.[15]

Wimsatt and Brooks quoted Lamb at his most impressionistic in his comment on *The Revenger's Tragedy,* but even here other considerations require attention. Lamb wrote:

The reality and life of this Dialogue passes any scenical illusion I ever felt. I never read it but my ears tingle, and I feel a hot blush spread my cheeks, as if I were presently about to 'proclaim' some such 'malefactions' of myself as the Brothers here rebuke in their unnatural parent; in words more keen and dagger-like than those which Hamlet speaks to his mother. Such power has the passion of shame truly personated, not only to 'strike guilty creatures unto the soul', but to 'appal' even those that are 'free'. (IV, 160).

This involved critical judgement as well as sensibility. Lamb claimed that his reading of Tourneur's dramatic poetry generated a more intense sympathetic identification than anything that he had ever experienced in the theatre. This comparison between the reading and the theatrical response re-appeared in his exploration of the aesthetic issues related to stage performance of Shakesperean tragedy. The Shakespearean tragic hero roused Lamb's imagination and sympathy more acutely in a reading than in a stage performance. Tourneur's dramatic poetry demanded a deep involvement of the reader's mind, and when Lamb expressed his physical reactions he sought to explain the affinity of his response with that of the dramatic character. Moreover, he also introduced a second literary context. The situation between Hamlet and Gertrude provided an appropriate reference as well as the vocabulary to weld the association, so that it seemed an integral part of his response and not an artificial appendage. The adjective 'unnatural' had a strength in the contexts of both plays. Hamlet vowed to 'be cruel, not unnatural', and Vindici addressed his mother as 'Wicked unnatural parent!' (IV, 158). There were other links. Hamlet said that he would 'speak daggers to her, but use none', and Vindici advised Hippolito to 'house' his 'dagger'. And just as Hamlet employed the Players to detect the guilt of Claudius, because he had

> heard
> That guilty creatures, sitting at a play,
> Have by the very cunning of the scene
> Been struck so to the soul that presently
> They have proclaim'd their malefactions,[16]

51

so in *The Revenger's Tragedy* the 'reality and life of this Dialogue' made Lamb react to the reproach, as intensely as did Vindici's mother. Quotations and allusions to *Hamlet* enabled Lamb to elucidate the effect of the poetry of *The Revenger's Tragedy*. Indeed, Lamb referred to Shakespeare very frequently in his notes. He compared Middleton and Shakespeare and argued that whereas Middleton's witches were 'creatures to whom man or woman plotting some dire mischief might resort for occasional consultation' Shakespeare's 'orginate deeds of blood, and begin bad impulses to men. From the moment that their eyes first meet with Macbeth's, he is spellbound. That meeting sways his destiny. He can never break the fascination' (IV, 144). The distinctions between the witches revealed the differences in imaginative conception between the plays of Middleton and Shakespeare. In this, as in the comment on *The Revenger's Tragedy* Lamb combined sensibility and critical intelligence.

Like Lamb, both Hazlitt and Coleridge valued instinct as a part of the critical response. Hazlitt argued that the 'intuitive perception of the hidden analogies of things, or, as it may be called, this *instinct of the imagination* . . . works unconsciously, like nature, and receives its impressions from a kind of inspiration' (VI, 109). In his *Spirit of the Age* he attacked Gifford because he thought that Gifford's criticism 'inclines, by a natural and deliberate bias, to the traditional in laws and government; to the orthodox in religion; to the safe in opinion; to the trite in imagination; to the technical in style; to whatever implies a surrender of individual judgement into the hands of authority, and a subjection of individual feeling to mechanic rules' (XI, 117). Lamb's comments in the *Specimens* showed a similar distaste for such qualities. His criticism elevated individual feeling and individual judgement (the combination was essential) to a position of dominant influence. He refused the impositions and restrictions of any so-called authority. Patmore wrote that Lamb 'spoke of Dryden's prefaces as the finest pieces of *criticism* . . . that had ever been written, and the better for being contradictory to each other, because not founded on any pretended rules'.[17]

Lamb believed that he had a 'suggestive' rather than a 'comprehensive' mind (II, 59), and thus he did not write any systematic criticism. He did not believe in it, and shared the antagonism of Keats and Hazlitt towards the tendency to systematize. Hazlitt exposed the weakness of philosophical systems as follows:

Another rule in philosophising is . . . to know where to stop. A man, by great labour and sagacity, finds out one truth; but from the importunate craving of the mind to know all, he would fain persuade himself that this one truth includes all others. Such has been the error of almost all systems and system-makers, who lose the advantage of the conquests they have achieved by pushing them too far, and aiming at universal empire. (XX, 375).

Keats argued that the 'only means of strengthening one's intellect is to make up one's mind about nothing – to let the mind be a thoroughfare for all thoughts',[18] and the idea of 'negative capability' stemmed from this principle. Perry suggested that Lamb provided the source of this idea and that he influenced Hazlitt who in turn influenced Keats.[19] Lamb grouped himself with those for whom 'Hints and glimpses, germs and crude essays at a system, is the utmost they pretend to . . . They are no systematizers, and would but err more by attempting it' (II, 59). Northrop Frye regarded Lamb as a public critic to whom a reader turned in order to '"appreciate" literature and get more direct contact with it', and the public critic

represents the reading public at its most expert and judicious. It is the task of the public critic to exemplify how a man of taste uses and evaluates literature, and thus show how litera-ture is to be absorbed into society. But here we no longer have the sense of an impersonal body of consolidating knowledge. The public critic tends to episodic forms like the lecture and the familiar essay, and his work is not a science, but another kind of literary art. He has picked up his ideas from a prag-matic study of literature, and does not try to create or enter into a theoretical structure.[20]

Hazlitt defined taste as 'the highest degree of sensibility, of the impression made on the most cultivated and sensible of minds' (IV, 164), and Lamb's taste rested upon the basis of wide and intelligent reading. In a letter to Southey on 10 February 1808 Coleridge praised the 'excellent Taste' of the *Specimens* and in a letter to Godwin on 21 May 1800 he argued that Lamb's 'taste acts so as to appear like the unmechanic simplicity of an Instinct – in brief, he is worth a hundred men of *mere* Talents'.[21]

III Lamb as Dramatist

Lamb's plays reflect interests which reappear in his criticism. In *Charles Lamb and Elia* J. E. Morpurgo rightly suggested that Lamb's 'dramatic efforts added to his academic knowledge, and gave to his criticism an element of practical appreciation that is rare save among exponents'.[1] The plays failed but Lamb's awareness of their weaknesses could heighten his sensitivity to similar faults in other writers, and this applied particularly to matters of plot and the organization of material. The plays also manifest his passion for the Elizabethan and Jacobean dramatists, and in *John Woodvil* and *The Wife's Trial* he imitated their style. Just as the *Specimens* and *Extracts* attempted to illustrate some of the qualities of these older dramatists so perhaps did *John Woodvil* and *The Wife's Trial.* The tragi-comedy of *The Wife's Trial,* written in 1827 and published in *Blackwood's Edinburgh Magazine* in December 1828, coincided with Lamb's selections from the Garrick Plays which appeared in William Hone's *Table Book* throughout 1827. Lamb claimed in a letter to Bernard Barton on 28 August 1827 that *The Wife's Trial* was in 'blank verse, and I think, of the true old dramatic cut' (*Letters*, III, 122). Although his enthusiasm for the theatre prompted him to write four plays, these works lacked the seriousness of mind which distinguished his criticism.

The plan which he conceived for *John Woodvil* combined qualities which distinguished many fine plays of the Elizabethan period. In a letter to Southey on 28 November 1798 he wrote:

> My Tragedy will be a medley (or I intend it to be a medley) of laughter and tears, prose and verse, and in some places rhyme, songs, wit, pathos, humour, and, if possible, sublimity; at least, it is not a fault in my intention, if it does not comprehend most of these discordant colours. Heaven send they dance not the 'Dance of Death!'

> (*Letters*, I, 141)[2]

Lamb recognized the nature of his material as so many 'discordant colours' but he failed to organize it. In his essay 'On the Genius and Character of Hogarth' published in 1811 he praised both Hogarth and Chaucer for that 'comprehensiveness of genius which could crowd, as poet and painter have done, into one small canvas so many diverse yet co-operating materials' (I, 77), and in his criticism of Shakespeare he shared Coleridge's judgement on the organic unity of Shakespearean tragedy, but in *John Woodvil* he could not combine the diverse elements into a unified work. He attempted to improve the organization of the play by the revisions which he made in 1801 before publication the following year, and he acknowledged in a letter to Rickman: 'I have long smelt a jumble. I hope you will find it now nearly all of a piece' (*Letters*, I, 287), but he did not succeed. In his composition of plays he could not embody those principles which controlled his comments in his criticism.

The manner in which he wrote to Southey in January 1799 of the composition of the play suggests that he held in his mind no clearly defined dramatic structure for it: 'I have only one slight passage to send you, scarce worth the sending, which I want to edge in somewhere into my play, which, by the way, hath not received the addition of ten lines, besides, since I saw you' (*Letters*, I, 146). He wrote fragments of poetry and prose and sought to put them together to form a play. His art of plotting stood at the furthest remove from what Fergusson called the Racinian technique of 'rational demonstration'.[3] Lamb's undisciplined plot lacked shape. The events of *John Woodvil* occur in an episodic manner. Yet tragedy demands a degree of inevitability, and it needs a carefully structured and developed action. A plot which unfolds merely by a series of accidents evokes no tragic mood, and this weakness marred *John Woodvil*. It lacked any sense of characters struggling with forces greater than themselves which appeared in Shakespearean tragedy. The characters lacked convincing motivation, and Southey had just reason to criticize the 'story' as 'very defective'.[4] Lamb's hero committed 'an error merely and no crime' (V, 167). This heightened the pathetic effect of the character but it did not make him tragic. Lamb lacked the dramatic skill to create interesting plots, and he never overcame this weakness, even when as in *The Wife's Trial* he borrowed his story from Crabbe's tale of 'The Confidant'. In a letter to Mrs Shelley on 26 July 1827 he freely acknowledged his inability to construct dramatic plots and to handle his characters:

I am busy with a farce in two acts, the incidents tragi-comic. I can do the dialogue *commey fo:* but the damned plot – I believe I must omit it altogether. The scenes come after one another like geese, not marshalling like cranes or a Hyde Park review. . . .

I want some Howard Paine to sketch a skeleton of artfully succeeding scenes through a whole play, as the courses are arranged in a cookery book: I to find wit, passion, sentiment, character, and the like trifles: to lay in the dead colours, – I'd Titianesque 'em up: to mark the channel in a cheek (smooth or furrowed, yours or mine), and where tears should course I'd draw the waters down: to say where a joke should come in or a pun be left out: to bring my *personae* on and off like a Beau Nash; and I'd Frankenstein them there: to bring three together on the stage at once; they are so shy with me, that I can get no more than two; and there they stand till it is the time, without being the season, to withdraw them.

(Letters, III, 110)

He did not lack imaginative power, but nowhere did formal organization characterize his work, not even in his best Elian essays. Richard Haven suggested that Lamb was 'no mean master of the Romantic idiom' which, he claimed, distinguished in particular Wordsworth and Coleridge; and he explained this idiom as 'a careful and artful poetic structure' in which 'we are presented not with a rationally ordered sequence but with a psychologically ordered movement of consciousness'.[5] Drama needs formal organization, but whilst Lamb's critical judgement recognized the problem he could not solve it in his own plays. In *The World of Elia* Fred V. Randel recently drew attention to De Quincey's emphasis on the discontinuity of the Elian essays. De Quincey wrote: 'The least observing reader of *Elia* cannot have failed to notice that the most felicitous passages always accomplish their circuit in a few sentences. The gyration within which his sentiment wheels, no matter of what kind it may be, is always the shortest possible. It does not prolong itself – it does not repeat itself – it does not propagate itself'. Randel argued that 'the inner necessities of Lamb's imaginative world make a discontinuous manner an expressive form. At the root of discontinuity in Lamb's greatest work is his understanding of human time'. Perhaps Lamb's 'discontinuous and abrupt' mind (again De Quincey's phrase) suited the essay but not drama.[6]

Lamb's admiration for the dramatic language of the Elizabethans and Jacobeans encouraged him to imitate them, and both he and Coleridge wrongly supposed that they could succeed with such language. Coleridge claimed: 'I tried to imitate his [Shakespeare's] manner in the Remorse, and when I had done, I found that I had been tracking Beaumont and Fletcher, and Massinger instead'.[7] Lamb defended his views in a letter to Southey in late January or early February 1799:

> You have read old Wither's Supersedeas to small purpose. You object to my pauses being at the end of my lines. I do not know any great difficulty I should find in diversifying or changing my blank verse; but I go upon the model of Shakspeare in my Play, and endeavour after a colloquial ease and spirit, something like him. I could so easily imitate Milton's versification; but my ear & feeling would reject it, or any approaches to it, in the *drama*. . . .
>
> I love to anticipate charges of unoriginality: the first [third] line is almost Shakspeare's: –
>
> 'To have my love to bed & to arise' *Midsummer Night's Dream* [III. i. 174]
>
> I think there is a sweetness in the versification not unlike some rhymes in that exquisite play. (*Letters,* I, 148-9).

Lamb referred to these lines:

> What sports do you use in the forest? –
> Not many; some few, as thus: –
> To see the sun to bed, and to arise,
> Like some hot amourist with glowing eyes. (V, 153)

The contrast between Lamb and Shakespeare emerged clearly in the line which Lamb pointed to as closely following Shakespeare. Lamb lost the pun and he lost the vital energy behind the line. His dramatic language lacked force. Many commentators, however, have acknowledged its beauty. Southey wrote that 'The last lines . . . are some of the finest that ever I remember and the whole is full of beauty'.[8] In 1820 the *Retrospective Review* commented that in *John Woodvil* the 'old English feeling of tender beauty has at last begun to revive. . . . Here, first, after a long interval, instead of the pompous swellings of inane declamation, the music of humanity was heard in its sweetest tones. The air of freshness breathed over its forest scenes, the delicate grace of its images'.[9] Hazlitt also wrote very favourably:

The defective or objectionable parts of this production are imitations of the defects of the old writers: its beauties are his own, though in their manner. The touches of thought and passion are often as pure and delicate as they are profound; and the character of his heroine Margaret is perhaps the finest and the most genuine female character out of Shakespear. (VI, 346).

But Lamb's dramatic language did not take account of the demands of his contemporary audiences. Visual effects were the most sought after and achieved the most success in the large London theatres, but Lamb wrote in an antiquated language, and audiences did not respond well to the poetic qualities of the plays offered to them. The style of *John Woodvil* reflected Lamb's absorption in Elizabethan and Jacobean literature and contrasted with the preference for a language closer to common life which Wordsworth advocated for poetry in his preface to the second edition of the *Lyrical Ballads*.[10] Hazlitt referred to Godwin's search among the Elizabethan dramatists in order to discover the author of a passage which Lamb had written.[11]

Despite the admiration for the beauty which characterized the poetry in *John Woodvil,* Lamb's limited poetic abilities could fail him and he could produce artificiality when he presented scenes of extreme passion. For instance, when Sir Walter realises that his son has betrayed him he dies of a broken heart, but whilst the reader's mind possibly recalls the pathos of Lear's end, Sir Walter speaks not one sentence in this scene and only a few phrases from Simon accompany his death (V, 165-7). The reader's feelings remain virtually untouched at what should be a moment of great emotional intensity. Lamb's verse rarely generated genuine emotion. The imagery in the speech beginning 'To see the sun to bed and to arise' assumed an essentially decorative role. It lacked the close poetic logic which Coleridge had admired in Shakespeare, and which he claimed to have learnt at Christ's Hospital where Boyer had taught that poetry 'even of the loftiest and seemingly, that of the wildest odes, had a logic of its own, as severe as that of science'.[12]

59

Lamb concentrated on the minds of his characters. Just as his critical comments on Shakespearean characters stressed that they were 'objects of meditation' so his plays presented the thoughts rather than deeds of the characters. Reading a Shakespearean tragedy revealed, for example, 'the texture of Othello's mind, the inward construction marvellously laid open with all its strengths and weaknesses' (I, 102)[13], and in the *Specimens* Lamb praised Ford because he 'sought for sublimity, not by parcels in metaphors or visible images, but directly where she has her full residence in the heart of man; in the actions and sufferings of the greatest minds' (IV, 218). However, Lamb sacrificed too much stage effect in favour of the exploration of the thoughts of his characters. He allowed them scant opportunity for action, and John Woodvil reveals his character mostly through soliloquy. In the letter to Rickman in 1801 which commented on the revisions to the play Lamb claimed that he had hoped to provide some 'relief to the oppression of John so often *talking* in his own person' (*Letters,* I, 286). John's reflections slow the play down; he talks mostly of the past, and his fine phrases do not stimulate interest in the development of the plot. He fails to rouse the reader's emotions, and he appears too insipid to lead the hearty and profligate life claimed for him. He lacks colour. At the close of the play he suffers an excess of guilt and appears truly repentant like the typical young prodigal of sentimental drama:

> O lady, poor and abject are my thoughts,
> My pride is cured, my hopes are under clouds,
> I have no part in any good man's love,
> In all earth's pleasures portion have I none,
> I fade and wither in my own esteem,
> This earth holds not alive so poor a thing as I am.
> I was not always thus. (V, 172).

In a letter to Manning of 28 December 1799 Lamb vigorously defended his original choice of *Pride's Cure* for the play's title, and added: 'I meant his punishment not alone to be a cure for his daily and habitual *pride,* but the direct consequence and appropriate punishment of a particular act of pride' (*Letters,* I, 167). He imposed this idea in the text rather blatantly. Margaret spoke of

one misfortune, child of chance,
No crime, but unforeseen, and sent to punish
The less offence with image of the greater,
Thereby to work the soul's humility,
(Which end hath happily not been frustrate quite).
(V, 172).

Despite Lamb's claims to have omitted 'a hodge-podge of German puerilities' (*Letters*, I, 305) in the revision of the play, the effusive humanitarian feelings in the closing scenes resemble the spirit of the German dramatist Kotzebue, whose popularity at the end of the eighteenth century in England exceeded that of Goethe and Schiller. The tastes of these eighteenth-century audiences did not earn the respect of twentieth-century commentators like Nicoll who argued that Kotzebue's influence in no way benefitted English drama. His 'romantic successes . . . only served to intensify that spectacular melodrama which was all that the new movement had to offer in the playhouse'.[14]

The first version of the play included 'scenes which shew'd John under the first impression of his father's death' and these were the scenes which included 'a hodge-podge of German puerilities'. In his letter to Rickman the reasons which Lamb gave for the omissions were consistent with comments which later appeared in his criticism. He explained the omissions as follows: 'I have done this, because I had made him too weak, and to expose himself before his servants, which was an indecorum; and from a theory that poetry has nothing to do to give *pain;* the imbecilities, and deformities, the dotages of human nature, are not fit objects to be shewn' (*Letters*, I, 286). His attention to decorum in literature manifested itself in his critical comments in the *Specimens;* and his belief in the principle that poetry should not cause pain influenced his comment in the essay on Shakespearean tragedy where he regretted that in stage performance 'the too close pressing semblance of reality, give a pain and an uneasiness which totally destroy all the delight which the words in the book convey, where the deed doing never presses upon us with the painful sense of presence' (I, 106). The emphasis on the painful here depended upon his perception of the different responses generated by a reading and a stage performance of a Shakespearean tragedy. Lamb objected when the stage performance caused a painful response. His opposition to the presentation of 'the imbecilities, and deformities, the dotages of human nature' influenced his comments on comedy. He did not believe that the stage should exploit human weaknesses which could not be altered, and in the Elian essay 'On Some of the Old Actors' he argued that Malvolio's 'pride, or his gravity, (call it which you will) is inherent, and native to the man, not mock or affected, which latter only are the fit objects to excite laughter' (II, 134). Comedy might correct man's affected but not his natural weaknesses.

Lamb did not possess the skill to delineate convincing dramatic characters. Of those in *John Woodvil* Margaret excites most interest. She at least makes decisions and acts upon them, as when she will not sacrifice her dignity by remaining in Woodvil's house where she is insulted. She explains to the faithful old steward Sandford that John and his companions treat her with contempt:

> Each day I endure fresh insult from the scorn
> Of Woodvil's friends, the uncivil jests,
> And free discourses, of the dissolute men,
> That haunt this mansion, making me their mirth.
>
> (V, 138).

She has too much self-respect to 'wait/The opportunity of a gracious hearing' from John Woodvil, and so she decides to leave the house and seek out Sir Walter in Sherwood Forest. In these early scenes she never appears on stage with either John Woodvil or his friends, but I feel that such a meeting could have produced theatrically effective dialogue. One of the Elizabethan or Jacobean dramatists whom Lamb admired might not have let go such an opportunity. Lamb described situations rather than create them dramatically. Margaret, however, has much of the spirit, if not the wit and gaiety, of Shakespearean heroines. She disguises herself in boy's costume just as Rosalind did in *As You Like It,* although Lamb ignored the convention whereby the disguise successfully concealed the character's true identity and he allowed Margaret to be recognized at once. There are more respects in which *John Woodvil* resembles *As You Like It* and Lott has pointed them out. They are the setting of Hall and forest and the eulogy on country life, the situations of Sir Walter and Duke

Senior, the estranged brothers, and the faithful servants Sandford and Adam, and just as Margaret marries John so Celia will marry Oliver.[15] In his letter to William Godwin on 17 September 1801 Lamb had stated: 'I am for introducing situations, sort of counter-parts to situations, which have been tried in other plays – *like* but not the *same*' (*Letters*, I, 276).

In December 1799 Lamb submitted the play to John Philip Kemble, but dramatists could not rely upon the efficient co-opera-tion of the managers, as Lamb soon learnt to his cost. Kemble lost the first copy of the play, and Lamb had to send a second version before he finally received an answer as to whether the play could or could not be acted at Drury Lane. On 3 November 1800 he wrote to Manning:

At last I have written to Kemble, to know the event of my play, which was presented last Christmas. As I suspected, came an answer back that the copy was lost, and could not be found – no hint that anybody had to this day ever looked into it – with a courteous (reasonable!) request of another copy (if I had one by me,) and a promise of a definite answer in a week. (*Letters,* I, 221).

However, the justice of Kemble's eventual decision cannot be questioned. Although Lamb considered submitting the play to Colman the Younger, who was then manager of the Haymarket theatre, whether he did so or not remains unknown. Unable to stage the play he printed it at his own cost and lost £25 in the process.[16] According to Southey both he and Coleridge tried to dissuade Lamb from publication but nevertheless Coleridge wrote in a letter to Godwin in December 1800 that 'at every perusal my love and admiration of his [Lamb's] Play rises a peg', and Southey was annoyed by Thomas Brown's attack on the play in *The Edinburgh Review.*[17] Apart from a fair review in *The Monthly Mirror* Lamb received contemptuous treatment from the periodical press. John Ferriar attacked the play in *The Monthly Review* and unfavourable criticism also appeared in *The Annual Review, The British Critic,* and *The Monthly Magazine. The Annual Review* seized the opportunity to enlarge its review into a general attack on the new 'school for poetry' which had been 'set up by Mr Lamb, and some others'.[18]

Three years later in September 1805 Lamb wrote to Wordsworth: 'I have done nothing since the beginning of last year, when I lost my newspaper job, and having had a long idleness, I must do something, or we shall get very poor. Sometimes I think of a farce' (*Letters,* I, 401). He completed his first farce *Mr H* in 1806, and it became the only one of his plays to be performed on the contemporary stage. This raised expectations of a good financial return. He explained to Manning on 5 December 1806; 'I shall get £200 from the theatre if "Mr H" has a good run, and I hope £100 for the copyright. Nothing if it fails' (*Letters,* II, 29). These hopes were not fulfilled because the play was damned upon the night of its first appearance on 10 December 1806 and not represented again. Although it was played with some success in the United States Lamb received no payment from those performances. W. R. Nethery showed that the play appeared at the Park Theatre, New York, on 16 March 1807, and again in 1817, 1825, and 1828. An 1817 edition of the *American Monthly Magazine and Critical Review* announced that the play had that year filled the house for Mr Hilson's benefit. *Mr H*'s greatest success probably came at the New Chestnut Theatre in Philadelphia, since the autobiography of the associate manager, William Wood, claimed that 'Charles Lamb's excellent farce of *Mr H* met with an extraordinary success, and was played an unusual number of nights'. The Chestnut Street Theatre also took the play on tour to Washington and Baltimore; and Nethery recorded other performances at Charleston, in 1807 and 1809, at Boston, in 1813, and at New Orleans, in 1824. In addition to this activity, two editions of the text were published in Philadelphia, the first in 1813 and the second in 1825.[19]

Both in *Mr H* and in his later farce *The Pawnbroker's Daughter* Lamb simply attempted to amuse an audience. He considered mere entertainment as one of the legitimate purposes of the theatre, and in a note in the *Specimens* he welcomed a scene in *The Merry Devil of Edmonton* which seemed 'written to make the Reader happy. Few of our dramatists or novelists have attended enough to this. . . . They are economists only in delight', and he argued that 'sweetness and good-naturedness' characterized 'Shakspeare's manner' (IV, 45). In his essay 'On the Artificial Comedy of the Last Century' he lamented the lost entertainment occasioned by the rarity of productions of plays by dramatists like Congreve, Farquhar, and Wycherley. The mood of *Mr H* is always good-humoured, just as in *The Pawnbroker's*

Daughter a reader does not believe that any harm can come from Flint's seemingly ruthless pursuit of justice. Lamb claimed to have written *Mr H* in 'mere wantonness of triumph' (*Letters,* II, 13) and although he might laugh in a genial way about the follies and pretensions of his characters, he did not expose them to satirical attack. There are no rapier thrusts in his wit and he rather concentrated upon exploiting his natural gift for puns and quibbles. He could write prose in a style deft and richly suggestive, and enriched by the peculiarities of his vocabulary. Jules Derocquigny described it as a style in which 'le mot arrete l'attention . . . Le mot, arrivant dans l'esprit de Lamb chargé de toutes les associations qu'il comporte, se fait sentir sur toute la phrase et sur les phrases qui suivent'.[20] Lamb abandoned the formal structuring that characterized late eighteenth-century writers like Gibbon. In a letter to Manning of 1 March 1800 in which he commented on Burnet's *History of His Own Times* he wrote that the work included 'none of the Damned philosophical Humeian indifference, so cold, and unnatural, and inhuman! None of the damned Gibbonian fine writing, so fine and composite! None of Mr Robertson's periods with three members' (*Letters,* I, 177). He employed language subtly, intertwining thoughts in an imaginative and idiosyncratic manner, creating an impression of spontaneity, imbuing his work with his personality, but firmly shaping his thoughts by his mastery of syntax and his acute use of his vocabulary. He misapplied his talents when he sought to produce farce which would satisfy the theatre audiences of the early nineteenth century. At that time farce succeeded by the broadest effects, by laughter and not by subtle wit. As in *John Woodvil* Lamb's style in *Mr H* was too literary for the large nineteenth-century theatres in which parts of the audience could neither see nor hear well. Stock characters and spectacular incidents dominated theatrical productions. Lamb perhaps realised this when he acknowledged that 'our nonsense did not happen to suit their nonsense' (I, 87).

He wrote *Mr H* as an afterpiece. It is, therefore, short, and it has a simple, straightforward story. Mr. H conceals his name because it presents an obstacle to marriage, and so simply as Mr H he begins a courtship with Melesinda. When he accidentally discovers his name as Hogsflesh the ladies reject him but he is reconciled with Melesinda when a royal warrant enables him to take the name of Bacon. Lamb acknowledged that the play hovered precariously between success and failure: 'there never was a more ticklish thing. The whole depends on the manner in which the name is brought out, which I value myself on, as a *chef d'oeuvre*' (*Letters,* II, 29). Brander Matthews proposed one reason for the play's failure when he argued that Lamb should not have kept the name a secret, since it provoked the audience to speculation and since to 'keep a secret is a misconception of true theatrical effect, an improper method of sustaining dramatic suspense'.[21] Nicoll rejected this idea. He stressed *Mr H*'s 'finer tone' which did not suit the London theatres, and also argued that 'the audiences of Lamb's time were becoming, not only prurient, but suspicious of anything that seemed "vulgar". When Mr H reveals himself as Hogsflesh, the very name, we must feel, grated on the supersensitive ears of the spectators and the hissing began'.[22] Nicoll believed that the farce would otherwise have succeeded.

After *Mr H*'s disastrous night Lamb informed Wordsworth of his misfortune in a letter of 11 December. He acknowledged his doubts about the play's potential:

I had many fears; the subject was not substantial enough. John Bull must have solider fare than a *Letter*. We are pretty stout about it, have had plenty of condoling friends, but after all, we had rather it should have succeeded. You will see the Prologue in most of the Morning Papers. It was received with such shouts as I never witness'd to a Prologue. It was attempted to be encored. How hard! a thing I did merely as a task, because it was wanted – and set no great store by; and Mr H–!!

The quantity of friends we had in the house, my brother and I being in Public Offices, &c. was astonishing – but they yielded at length to a few hisses. A hundred hisses – damn the word, I write it like kisses – how different – a hundred hisses outweigh a 1000 Claps. The former come more directly from the Heart – Well, 'tis withdrawn and there is an end. (*Letters,* II, 31).

However well he may have tried to laugh off his failure he could not rid himself of his disappointment and anger, although neither he nor Mary sought to blame anyone else for the play's failure. Mary wrote to Mrs Clarkson on 23 December 1806; 'I do not love to throw the blame of the ill success of a piece upon the actors – it is a common trick with unsuccessful dramatists. The blame rested chiefly with Charles, and yet should not be called blame, for it was mere ignorance of stage effect' (*Letters,* II, 32). Lamb fully accepted responsibility for the play's weakness, but what rankled and what later stimulated his essay 'On the Custom of Hissing at the Theatre' was his conviction that he had committed no offence which deserved such savage treatment: 'I could not help asking, what crime of great moral turpitude I had committed: for every man about me seemed to feel the offence as personal to himself, as something which public interest and private feelings alike called upon him in the strongest possible manner to stigmatise with infamy' (I, 89). In his own view his 'demerit' was simply that of one who 'thought to please us in the act of filling his pockets', and he described this as a 'venial mistake'. The essay mixed humour and vicious anger. Lamb shared, if only momentarily, Byron's sensitivity to the vulnerability of an author who put his work on the stage. Byron declared that he wrote *Manfred* 'with a *horror* of the stage, and with a view to render even the thought of it impracticable, knowing the zeal of my friends that I should try that for which I have an invincible repugnance, viz. a representation'.[23] Lamb responded to the treatment of *Mr H* with an outburst of deeply wounded feelings, and he struck back fiercely. He felt unjustly treated. In the *Specimens* he quoted Webster's comment on 'the uncapable multitude' (IV, 181) and there were occasions on which he shared that opinion:

> The public, or mob, in all ages, have been a set of blind, deaf, obstinate, senseless, illiterate savages . . . no man of genius in his senses would be ambitious of pleasing such a capricious, ungrateful rabble . . . the only legitimate end of writing for them is to pick their pockets, and, *that failing,* we are at full liberty to vilify and abuse them as much as ever we think fit. (I, 91).

J. B. Priestley suggested that most dramatists at some point in their careers launch a diatribe which denounces the incompetent judgement of theatre audiences.[24] It is their retaliation against judgements which admit of no appeal. But Lamb's reaction took root in a principle and it cannot be dismissed as simply emotional. He disliked aggressive, destructive criticism. He objected to 'your obstreperous talking critics, – the impertinent guides of the pit, – who will not give a plain man leave to enjoy an evening's entertainment, but with their frothy jargon, and incessant finding of faults, either drown his pleasure quite, or force him in his own defence to join in their clamorous censure' (I, 90). He resented the captious. His open-minded approach to the theatre determined the experience, rich in variety and quality, which he drew from it. He appreciated entertainment whether it was offered by Shakespeare or farcical pantomime, and he abhorred the cant of critics who obtruded their esoteric or fashionable notions upon the audiences.

Lamb wrote his second farce, *The Pawnbroker's Daughter,* in 1825 and it was published in *Blackwood's Edinburgh Magazine* in January 1830. The story of the pawnbroker Flint and his daughter Marian resembled but significantly differed from the story of Shylock and Jessica in *The Merchant of Venice.* Whereas Jessica deliberately took Shylock's jewels, Marian left home with her suitor Davenport in such haste and confusion that she quite inadvertently made off with the casket which Flint had entrusted to her, and she attempted to return it through Maria Flyn. Flint believed that she had stolen the casket and a warrant was issued for her arrest, but Maria Flyn was arrested by mistake. Flint scorned the Justice's entreaty for compassion and demanded that 'the law take its course', just as Shylock insisted: 'I crave the law', but where Shylock pursued a pound of Antonio's flesh Flint sought a judgement against his daughter. Flint's claim 'I am a rock, absolute rock, to all that you can say – A piece of solid rock' became ridiculous by the acknowledgement which immediately followed this: 'What is it that makes my legs to fail, and my whole frame to totter thus? It has been my over walking. I am very faint. Support me in, William' (V, 229). Shylock's lack of compassion far exceeded Flint's. At the close of *The Pawnbroker's Daughter* Flint is reconciled with Davenport and Marian, but no reconciliation occurs in *The Merchant of Venice;* and when in the last words of the play Flint announced that he valued 'one poor domestic jewel' (V, 242), Marian, more than the jewels in the casket, he reversed Shylock's alleged priorities. Lamb wrote a good-humoured play with a happy ending, and again he exploited plays on words as well as the occasional literary joke. When Pendulous was arrested as a pickpocket he gave a false name, that of James Thomson.

In 1827 Lamb wrote his fourth and final play, the tragi-comedy entitled *The Wife's Trial,* though without expectation of a success which in this genre always eluded him. On 19 July he wrote to P. G. Patmore: 'I am doing a tragi-comedy in two acts, and have got on tolerably, but it will be refused, or worse. I never had luck with any thing my name was put to' (*Letters,* III, 105). He submitted the play to Charles Kemble in 1827 and it met with the rejection which he had feared. Those faults of plot and characterisation which had weakened *John Woodvil* reappeared in *The Wife's Trial,* and again he imitated the style of the Elizabethan and Jacobean dramatists. In some of the scenes between Selby and Mrs Frampton he also used that common device of those older dramatists whereby a character spoke his mind in jests, riddles, or under the cloak of an assumed third person. Shakespeare's plays contained many significant instances of 'seeming', and in *The Wife's Trial* Selby's sister Lucy advocated 'For honest ends, a most dishonest seeming' (V, 257). Selby acknowledged his 'honest seeming' and 'seeming courtship', whilst Mrs Frampton put on a 'riddling veil' (V, 262-3).

Lamb took the story for the play from Crabbe's tale of 'The Confidant' from the *Tales* published in 1812, but he made changes in Crabbe's plot and weakened it. Crabbe began with a portrayal of Anna's youth, elucidating the essential characteristics of her nature, and revealing the 'offence' which she has committed, whereas Lamb began at a much later stage in his heroine's life, concealing the 'offence' and thus attempting to gain interest and suspense. He had used this technique unsuccessfully in *Mr H,* and in *The Wife's Trial* it also failed. When Lamb ultimately informed his audience of the secret he left them with a sense of anti-climax. In Crabbe's tale, since the reader understands the relationship between Anna and Eliza before they confront each other in the same house, Crabbe could exploit the tension and dramatic possibilities of the situation:

> They sate one evening, each absorb'd in gloom,
> When, hark! a noise and rushing to the room,
> The Friend tripp'd lightly in, and laughing said, 'I come'.[25]

The slow movement of the first line with its long vowel sounds conveys the doleful atmosphere of the household, and then the silence is broken by the noise of the friend's arrival, which is reflected in the syntactical structure, 'When, hark! a noise'. In the longer twelve syllable last line the heavy caesura and the decisive position of 'I come', occupying the two extra syllables, reinforce the impact of Eliza's arrival and add an air of menace. Crabbe created a rich and powerful language which provided dramatic effect. He wrote emphatically, with a strength and economy and a very positive control of the syntax and structure of his verse. He suited the framework of the heroic couplet to his own needs, and he gained force from his end-stopped lines, his internal pauses, and his antitheses:

> The husband doubted; he was kind but cool: –
> ''Tis a strong friendship to arise at school;
> Once more then, love, once more the sufferer aid, –
> I too can pity, but I must upbraid;
> Of these vain feelings then thy bosom free,
> Nor be o'erwhelm'd by useless sympathy.'   (319–24).

This recalls the manner of some earlier Augustan poetry, whereas Lamb's verse expresses ideas with less brevity and moves more freely. In the following lines Selby expresses deeply felt emotions but they are much gentler than those in Crabbe's tale:

> I was to caution you
> Against this fault of a too grateful nature:
> Which, for some girlish obligations past,
> In that relenting season of the heart,
> When slightest favours pass for benefits
> Of endless binding, would entail upon you
> An iron slavery of obsequious duty
> To the proud will of an imperious woman. (V, 244).

Crabbe's tale inspires a passionate and deeply serious response whilst in Lamb's play nothing stimulates a similar feeling. In 'The Confidant' Anna's feelings are vividly and convincingly developed and Eliza poses a real and genuine threat:

> All trace of comfort vanish'd if she spoke,
> The noisy friend upon her purpose broke;
> To her remarks with insolence replied,
> And her assertions doubted or denied;
> While the meek Anna like an infant shook,
> Wo-struck and trembling at the serpent's look.
>   (378–83).

70

The tale evokes a grim, serious mood in which Eliza's vindictiveness is countered by a fierce attempt at self-justification. Lamb's substitute for Eliza, Mrs Frampton, acts proudly and harshly but inclines more to sorrowful reflection upon her more fortunate past than to the despair and extreme poverty which drives Eliza. Lamb allows Mrs Frampton moments of feeling which were not a part of Eliza's character:

> Come, come,
> 'Twas something, or 'twas nothing, that I said;
> I did not mean to fright you, sweetest bed-fellow.'
>
> (V, 253).

Mrs Frampton is Lamb's most evil dramatic character but she is never really bad, whilst Katherine, the play's heroine, behaves so insipidly that she does not encourage as great a sympathy as Anna does. She is less fully realised than Anna.

Lamb reduced the seriousness of the story. He eliminated the blackmail; he introduced humour in the scene between the servants; and the end of the play revealed the same sentimentalism as had appeared in *John Woodvil*. Selby declares:

> Widow, your hand. I read a penitence
> In this dejected brow; and in this shame
> Your fault is buried. You shall in with us,
> And, if it please you, taste our nuptial fare:
> For, till this moment, I can joyful say,
> Was never truly Selby's Wedding Day. (V, 273).

A contrite Mrs Frampton receives complete forgiveness for her trangressions, but in Crabbe the end is inexorable:

> Twice made the Guest an effort to sustain
> Her feelings, twice resumed her seat in vain,
> Nor could suppress her shame, nor could support her pain:
> Quick she retired, and all the dismal night.
> Thought of her guilt, her folly, and her flight;
> Then sought unseen her miserable home,
> To think of comforts lost, and brood on wants to come.
>
> (584–90).

Crabbe could not countenance a different conclusion. Reconciliation at this point would have been an artificial imposition on the tale, whereas Lamb prepared for his sentimental close by the changes which enabled him to lighten a heavy atmosphere. Macdonald commented that 'in so far as Lamb innovated upon the story, he abolished rational motive, and so weakened its moral coherence and dramatic character'.[26] Crabbe was tough and unsentimental, with a grim philosophy of life, and his tales pursued inflexibly the consequences of the action. Although Hazlitt thought that 'The Confidant' was one of Crabbe's best tales, he strongly criticized the lack of balance which he found in Crabbe's treatment of mankind. Hazlitt claimed that Crabbe presented 'discoloured paintings of life; helpless, repining, unprofitable, unedifying distress' and he accused him of being 'not a philosopher, but a sophist, a misanthrope in verse; a *namby-pamby* Mandeville, a Malthus turned metrical romancer' (XI, 167), and in 'Conversations as Good as Real (2)' in *The Atlas* of 20 September 1829 he wrote that 'Crabbe is an original writer; but it is to be hoped he will have few followers. Mr Lamb, by softening the disagreeableness of one of his tales, has taken out the sting' (XX, 276). Crabbe's dire tone differed greatly from the attitudes of Lamb, who probably shared Hazlitt's antipathy to the Benthamite philosophy of psychological egoism. Altick suggested that the ideas of Lamb, Leigh Hunt, and Hazlitt contrasted with 'the orthodox Benthamite view'.[27] Both *John Woodvil* and *The Wife's Trial* suggest a positive and optimistic view of human nature. Lamb's plays expressed a spirit of reconciliation and benevolent emotions prevailed.

IV   Lamb as Critic of Theatrical Performance

In this chapter I shall comment upon Lamb's criticism on dramatic illusion, on actors and acting techniques, and on what he called 'artificial comedy'. In his comments on actors Lamb discussed two opposed acting techniques which, as W. E. Houghton suggested, might be described as 'natural' and 'artificial'. Lamb commented on the natural acting of Bensley, Fanny Kelly, and Mrs Jordan, and on the artificial acting of Bannister and Palmer, and in August 1825 when he published the essay entitled 'Stage Illusion' he presented his mature ideas on the relationship between these acting techniques and dramatic illusion. I also believe that these theories of acting determined the ideas in his essay 'On the Artificial Comedy of the Last Century' where he expressed his notorious judgement on the world of this comedy as 'altogether a speculative scene of things, which has no reference whatever to the world that is'.[1]

In 'Stage Illusion' Lamb did not refer to the concept of dramatic illusion as in any way connected with the elaborate scenery employed in contemporary attempts at verisimilitude in stage setting. He objected to the traditional method of judging how well a play was acted because he did not believe that the degree of scenical illusion produced could provide a sound basis for judgement. He did not concern himself with neo-classical ideas of the 'necessity of literal delusion'.[2] Lamb's experience as a spectator in the theatre progressively convinced him that different degrees of 'scenical illusion' were required by different dramatic genres, and that consequently a well-acted play was one in which the degree of scenical illusion produced was appropriate to the kind of play performed. Lamb distinguished between the scenical illusion demanded by a tragedy and that demanded by certain types of comedy, and his explanation of the idea stressed the central importance of the actor in establishing the illusion.

The actor who was usually thought to produce the best illusion was he who,

appears wholly unconscious of the presence of spectators. In tragedy – in all which is to affect the feelings – this undivided attention to his stage business, seems indispensable. . . . But, tragedy apart, it may be inquired whether, in certain characters in comedy, especially those which are a little extravagant, or which involve some notion repugnant to the moral sense, it is not a proof of the highest skill in the comedian when, without absolutely appealing to an audience, he keeps up a tacit understanding with them; and makes them, unconsciously to themselves, a party in the scene. (II, 163).

Lamb held in contempt those 'cleverest tragedians' who indulged in 'references to an audience' which hindered the successful performance of tragedy. The tragic actor had to involve himself in the role which he played in order to engage the emotional response of the spectators. If he destroyed the illusion then he deprived the audience of a full appreciation of the tragedy. Comedy required a more detached attitude of the audience, and an actor thus needed a different technique. In 'certain characters in comedy' an actor who manifested his consciousness of the audience and who made 'references' to them could very effectively improve his performance. Lamb discussed Bannister's manner of acting cowards and argued that such a character, if presented too realistically, would revolt an audience and so interfere with its pleasure. But Bannister acted a coward in such a manner that an audience did not find the character distasteful.

We loved the rogues. How was this effected but by the exquisite art of the actor in a perpetual sub-insinuation to us, the spectators, even in the extremity of the shaking fit, that he was not half such a coward as we took him for? . . . Was this a genuine picture of a coward? or not rather a likeness, which the clever artist contrived to palm upon us instead of an original; while we secretly connived at the delusion for the purpose of greater pleasure, than a more genuine counterfeiting of the imbecility, helplessness, and utter self-desertion, which we know to be concomitants of cowardice in real life, could have given us? (II, 163–4).

Bannister's deliberately non-natural acting ensured his success, because such characters 'please by being done under the life, or beside it; not *to the life*' (II, 164). Lamb explained the failure of Emery in comic roles as the consequence of that actor's application of acting techniques which had succeeded in his tragic roles

74

but which were totally unsuited to comic roles. Emery acted too naturally in his comic roles, for less credibility was required in comedy than in tragedy (II, 164–5).

Lamb's argument stressed that in certain representations an audience's pleasure depended upon their consciousness of the fiction. A similar point emerged in Shakespeare's *A Midsummer Night's Dream* where Quince, Bottom, Flute, Snout, Starveling and Snug decided not to maintain scenical illusion in their playing of the 'Pyramus and Thisbe' story. They acknowledged that they could not present an unpleasant character like the lion too realistically because it might frighten the lady spectators. Bottom suggests that Snug

> must name his name, and half his face must be seen through the lion's neck; and he himself must speak through, saying thus, or to the same defect: 'Ladies,' or 'Fair ladies, I would wish you' or 'I would request you' or 'I would entreat you not to fear, not to tremble. My life for yours! If you think I come hither as a lion, it were pity of my life. No, I am no such thing; I am a man as other men are'. And there, indeed, let me name his name, and tell them plainly he is Snug the joiner. (III. i. 25–40).

By deliberately unrealistic acting they could create an attitude of detachment, but it was only with Lamb that artificial and natural acting techniques were directly related to 'certain kinds of comedy' and to tragedy respectively.

ii

The essay 'On Some of the Old Actors' included Lamb's critical comments on Bensley's acting of Iago and Malvolio. He regarded Bensley's Iago as 'the only endurable' performance of that character which he had seen, and this judgement implicitly snubbed actors like Kean who enjoyed popular reputations in the second and third decades of the nineteenth century. Lamb remained virtually silent about Kean, but from Hazlitt's account of Kean's Iago it would appear that a gap existed between Lamb's conception of the ideal presentation of the character and Kean's

manner of acting it. Despite his admiration for Kean Hazlitt
reproached him for actions which were 'not the text of
Shakespear' (V, 221) and for 'the extreme alteration' of 'the
essence of the character'. Hazlitt expressed reservations on the
'pattern of comic gaiety and good-humour' (IV, 17) which Kean
introduced, and he argued that the weakest point of the performance appeared 'in the third act with Othello, where "comes the
tug of war"' (V, 219). He regretted that the 'deep internal work-
ing of hypocrisy under the mask of love and honesty, escaped us
on the stage' (V, 219–20), and thus Kean did not realize Lamb's
'consummate villain entrapping a noble nature into toils, against
which no discernment was available, where the manner was as
fathomless as the purpose seemed dark, and without motive' (II,
134), which was how Bensley played the character.

Bensley's acting displayed those qualities which Lamb connected with *natural* acting and which he regarded as essential for
the successful performance of characters in tragedy. Bensley was
'totally destitute of trick and artifice. He seemed come upon
the stage to do the poet's message simply, and he did it with as
genuine fidelity as the nuncios in Homer deliver the errands of
the gods'. He 'betrayed none of that *cleverness* which is the
bane of serious acting' (II, 133). He maintained scenical illusion
by a strict attention to his role, and did not engage in any 'by-
intimations to make the audience fancy their own discernment so
much greater than that of the Moor' (II, 134). *Artificial* acting
would have debased the grandeur of the struggle between Iago
and Othello. However, Bensley's style of natural acting also
seemed to influence his performance of Malvolio. Lamb made no
distinction between the acting techniques which Bensley used in
the roles of Iago and Malvolio, and the essay suggested that the
techniques were the same. Thus Bensley treated the role of
Malvolio as 'serious acting' (II, 133), and performed the character
'with a richness and a dignity' (II, 134).

Lamb's argument depended upon his sense of Malvolio's worth.
His belief that the man commanded a certain respect formed the
essence of his interpretation of the character, and a large part of
the essay aimed at substantiating that belief. He argued that
Malvolio was not a 'buffoon' but rather a man who earnt
responsibility and a measure of respect from his social superiors:
'He is master of the household to a great Princess; . . . Olivia, at

the first indication of his supposed madness, declares that she "would not have him miscarry for half of her dowry'" (II, 134–5). Lamb insisted that Malvolio should not be confused with the 'eternal old, low steward of comedy'. The 'true clown' in the play was Feste who jested for his living. Malvolio occupied a serious position.

Although Lamb respected what he believed to be Malvolio's 'estimable qualities' (II, 135) he did not regard him as a pleasant character. On the contrary, Malvolio was 'at the best unlovely'. He was 'cold, austere, repelling; . . . of an over-stretched morality . . . a sort of Puritan' (II, 134). Lamb fully realized that Malvolio behaved in a manner which was quite out of place in the world created by the inhabitants of Illyria, but that did not make Malvolio contemptible. His weaknesses were not affected, 'his superstructure of pride seemed bottomed upon a sense of worth. There was something in it beyond the coxcomb. It was big and swelling, but you could not be sure that it was hollow' (II, 135). Lamb did not consider Malvolio to be suitable for evoking laughter because his pride was 'inherent, and native to the man, not mock or affected, which latter only are the fit objects to excite laughter' (II, 134). He did not believe that comedy had anything to do with the ridiculing of an otherwise worthy man's incorrigible weaknesses, and so Malvolio 'becomes comic but by accident'. Thus Lamb did not argue for the complete exclusion of a comic response to Malvolio but he did insist that he was not 'essentially ludicrous'. His attitude can be clarified by reference to Congreve's letter to the 'Earl of Mountague' which prefaced *The Way of the World*.

Those Characters which are meant to be ridiculous in most of our Comedies, are of Fools so gross, that in my humble Opinion, they should rather disturb than divert the well-natur'd and reflecting part of an Audience; they are rather Objects of Charity than Contempt; and instead of moving our Mirth, they ought very often to excite our Compassion.

This Reflection mov'd me to design some Characters, which should appear ridiculous not so much thro' a natural Folly (which is incorrigible, and therefore not proper for the Stage) as thro' an affected Wit.[3]

By these criteria Lamb's Malvolio became a compassionate rather than a properly comic character. Lamb found that when Malvolio was at the height of his deception concerning the Countess's love, you were infected with the illusion, and did not wish that it should be removed! you had no room for laughter! if an unseasonable reflection of morality obtruded itself, it was a deep sense of the pitiable infirmity of man's nature, that can lay him open to such frenzies – but in truth you rather admired than pitied the lunacy while it lasted – you felt that an hour of such mistake was worth an age with the eyes open. (II, 135–6).

Lamb gave moral support to Malvolio's struggle to realize his dream and thus he could not patronise him. He acknowledged that feelings of pity were 'unseasonable' and thus inappropriate to this comedy, but instead of laughter he substituted admiration. Respect for Malvolio committed Lamb's sympathies: 'Who would not wish to live but for a day in the conceit of such a lady's love as Olivia?' (II, 136). The word 'conceit' suggested, on the one hand, the pride which he could not condemn in Malvolio, and on the other hand, the fine conception, the imaginative idea of such a love which Lamb enjoyed and which Bensley's abilities as an actor well suited – at least as Lamb described those abilities: 'Bensley had most of the swell of soul, was greatest in the delivery of heroic conceptions, the emotion consequent upon the present-ment of a great idea to the fancy. He had the true poetical enthusiasm – the rarest faculty among players' (II, 133).

Both Lamb and Hazlitt took Malvolio seriously, and in Hazlitt's response a close link existed between the respect and the sympathy which he had for Malvolio: 'we feel a regard for Malvolio, and sympathise with his gravity, his smiles, his cross garters, his yellow stockings, and imprisonment in the stocks' (IV, 315). As Barnet suggested, Hazlitt maintained the play on the level of comedy by his judgement that poetic justice finally reigned: 'If poor Malvolio's treatment afterwards is a little hard, poetical justice is done in the uneasiness which Olivia suffers on account of her mistaken attachment to Cesario, as her insensi-bility to the violence of the Duke's passion is atoned for by the discovery of Viola's concealed love of him' (IV, 318). Lamb did not admit poetic justice and so without this counter-balancing idea his emotional sympathies became deeply involved and prompted him to the declaration of a 'kind of tragic interest' in Malvolio's 'catastrophe'. The context clarified Lamb's idea since 'fate and retribution' will not permit Malvolio's usurped position to endure, and 'thus the whirligig of time . . . brings in his revenges' (II, 136). The notion of time here determined Lamb's recognition of the potentiality of tragedy in Malvolio. Northrop Frye suggested that the 'basis of the tragic vision is being in time', and this 'being in time is not the whole of the tragic vision: it is, in itself, the ironic vision. Because it is the basis of the tragic vision, the ironic and the tragic are often confused or identified'.[4] Lamb acknowledged that *Twelfth Night* did not develop into a tragedy, and that comedy maintained its rightful place, for if Malvolio threatened the comic world of Illyria, he did not succeed in upsetting it. 'He is opposed to the proper *levities* of the piece, and falls in the unequal contest' (II, 134). Malvolio met not a tragic but an ironic fate.

Lamb claimed to derive this interpretation of Malvolio from Bensley's acting, but he was only twenty-one years old when Bensley retired from the stage in 1796 and thus his memory was obliged to go back at least twenty-six years. The question of how much responsibility for the interpretation belonged to Lamb and how much to Bensley cannot be easily resolved, since few contemporary accounts of Bensley's acting exist. However, Sylvan Barnet claimed in his 'Charles Lamb and the Tragic Malvolio' that the interpretation belonged solely to Lamb and not at all to Bensley: 'The evidence of Bensley's contemporaries clearly suggests that the actor's Malvolio was not that which Lamb depicted twenty-six years after Bensley had retired.'[5] I do not find Barnet's evidence fully convincing.

The earliest commentator whom Barnet quoted was M. J. Young, whose *Memoirs of Mrs Crouch* appeared in 1806. Young was the only one of the writers whom Barnet quoted who wrote before Lamb's essay appeared in 1822. Barnet contrasted Lamb's Steward of 'richness and dignity' with Young's, 'Mr Bensley, in the vain fantastical Malvolio, was excellent',[6] but this comparison can be misleading because Lamb recognized that at a certain point in the play Malvolio lost much of his dignity:

> but when the decent sobrieties of the character began to give way, and the poison of self-love, in his conceit of the Countess's affection, gradually to work, you would have thought that the hero of La Mancha in person stood before you. How he went smiling to himself! with what ineffable carelessness would he twirl his gold chain! what a dream it was! (II, 135).

This was a 'vain' and a 'fantastical' Malvolio, and in these comments Lamb showed no real dissimilarity with the judgement of Young.

Barnet also quoted from the works of George Colman the Younger, John Taylor, and John Genest, who published their comments on Bensley in 1830, 1832, and 1832 respectively. All of these three writers limited themselves to observations which concerned Bensley's physical attributes and their suitability for the role of Malvolio. Barnet wrote:

John Taylor observed that 'his voice was rough, and had no variety' and its tones were 'grave and often nasal'. Bensley's stiffness was also mentioned frequently, but most commentators add that although he triumphed over these handicaps, they were not always liabilities. Genest wrote that 'his voice and manner were well suited to Malvolio', and Taylor said that all his pecularities 'operated in his favour in the part of Malvolio'. Similarly, George Colman the Younger held that Bensley's stalk, stiffness, and nasal twang aided him in 'his personification of Malvolio, the starch and conceited Steward'.[7]

Bensley's reputation for stiffness existed before he had ever played Malvolio. Some verse in the *Gentleman's Magazine* of January 1772 included the line: 'B was for Bensley, as stiff as you please.' Some of the comments which Barnet quoted bore an extraordinary resemblance rather than contrast with those of Lamb. Lamb wrote that Bensley's 'gait was uncouth and stiff', that he was 'starch, spruce, opinionated', and that his 'voice had the dissonance and at times the inspiriting effect of the trumpet'. But more important, and unquoted by Barnet, were Lamb's 'the thoroughbred gentleman was uppermost in every movement' (II, 133) and Colman's: 'Bensley, who always maintain'd an upper rank upon the stage, both in Tragedy and Comedy, was respectable in *all* the characters he undertook.'[8] Here there was more than a glimpse of Lamb's dignified Malvolio. In 1839 Adolphus referred to Bensley's 'solemn deportment'[9] which echoed Lamb's comment: 'His bearing is lofty. . . . He looked, spake, and moved like an old Castilian' (II, 134–5). These comments did not contradict Lamb.

Barnet argued that the 'dignity which Lamb felt invested Bensley, Bensley's contemporaries often felt was comic' and he quoted John Adolphus and James Boaden to support this statement. Adolphus wrote of Bensley's 'ludicrous gullibility in Malvolio';[10] and Boaden commented:

Bensley and Aiken were both manly; but for pleasantry, alas! it became *satire* in passing their lips. I never laughed with Bensley but once, and then he represented Malvolio, in which, I thought him perfection. Bensley had been a soldier, yet his stage walk eternally reminded you of the *'one, two, three, hop'* of the dancing-master; this scientific progress of legs, in yellow stockings, most villainously cross-gartered, with a horrible laugh of ugly conceit to top the whole, rendered him Shakespeare's Malvolio at all points.[11]

In order to support his recollection of the essential dignity of Malvolio Lamb pointed out that when Bensley could not act the role he was replaced by John Philip Kemble, an actor more respected for his tragic than for his comic acting. Lamb implied that Kemble, an actor of natural dignity, could most easily take over the role and play it in the manner established by Bensley. Kemble did not act buffoons. The only genuinely contemporary comment which I have found on the comic nature of the part appeared in *The Morning Chronicle, and London Advertiser* of 23 September 1782, where the reviewer wrote that 'Bensley happily hit off the dry and costive humour of Malvolio'. The words 'dry' and 'costive' did not imply that an audience experienced great amusement during Bensley's performance of Malvolio. Lamb's subjective response to Malvolio differed from that of Boaden and Adolphus, but Boaden wrote thirty-five years after Bensley's retirement and Adolphus forty-three. In the absence of a sufficient quantity of other evidence, their statements did not disprove Lamb's.

I have discovered only one instance in which another critic's comment on Bensley directly contradicted the objective attributes described by Lamb. In *The Gazetteer* of 27 June 1791 the theatrical reviewer claimed that Bensley had spoilt 'a performance otherwise good by concluding his sentences with a rant, and a look at the gallery (i.e. to invite applause)'. If Bensley did act in this manner then Lamb falsely praised his lack of 'trick and artifice', and the acting techniques consistent with Lamb's interpretation did not find their expression in Bensley. This supports Barnet's argument, and despite his lack of real evidence he perhaps reached a correct conclusion. However, Lamb described

Bensley with sufficient accuracy in respect of the well-known characteristics of the actor to disguise a possibly personal interpretation of Malvolio. Here Lamb combined theatrical and literary criticism, so that his imagination embodied a whole acting performance at the same time as his mind reasoned its critical analysis of the character.

iii

In Lamb's criticism of actors and acting techniques he revealed the imaginative qualities which distinguished his critical notes to the *Specimens* and *Extracts*. He showed an imaginative force which matched that of the actor discussed. In his essays on Munden and Dodd he displayed an acute sensibility to the individual distinguishing characteristics of those comic actors; and such criticism required the kind of perception which Hazlitt described as a response to all 'the infinite fluctuations of thought through their nicest distinctions' (II, 261), and in his view this 'trembling sensibility which is awake to every change and modification of its ever-varying impressions' (VIII, 83) characterized the poetic response. Lamb's criticism of actors gave evidence of such a poetic response.

The Athenaeum of 11 February 1832 acknowledged Lamb's particular skill in describing actors: 'others . . . have been embalmed, in all their vital spirit, by Elia himself; in whose unrivalled volume *Cockletop* is preserved as in amber, and where Munden will live for aye, making mouths at Time and Oblivion'. Lamb's criticism invested actors and actresses like Munden, Dodd, Bensley, Bannister, Mrs Jordan, and Fanny Kelly with a permanence which the nature of their art usually stole, a permanence which Lamb based not upon a record of details which could be visualized but on an appreciation of the 'vital spirit' which informed their acting. He penetrated to and reflected in his writing the essence of their acting, that which most stimulated his thoughts and feelings, that faculty of the actor which generated the expression of inner character.

The quality which Lamb found as central to Munden's acting

was gusto, a quality which Hazlitt also commented upon in that actor (XVIII, 223). Hazlitt once explained gusto in art as 'power or passion defining any object . . . it is in giving this truth of character from the truth of feeling, whether in the highest or the lowest degree, but always in the highest degree of which the subject is capable, that gusto consists'. He commented upon a lack of gusto as follows: 'Vandyke's flesh-colour, though it has great truth and purity, wants gusto. It has not the internal character, the living principle in it. It is a smooth surface, not a warm, moving mass' (IV, 77). It was precisely that internal character which Lamb perceived as one of the distinctions of Munden's acting when he declared: 'Now, *that* is not what I call *acting*. It might be better. He was imaginative; he could impress upon an audience an *idea*' (I, 342). Lamb stressed that Munden conveyed an apprehension of the essential rather than the external qualities of objects, which made of his acting a subjective art. Lamb's interest centred on the imaginative conception which informed the acting, and on the nature of the expression produced. He also applied these principles in his criticism of painting, discussed in the next chapter, and both Lamb and Hazlitt used the term gusto to comment on painting as well as the theatre. Roy Park quoted Hazlitt's comment on Kean that 'there is a tone in acting, as well as in painting, which is the chief and master excellence' (V, 184), and he added that 'this "tone" is intimately bound up with their common basis in expression'.[12]

Lamb found a gusto in Munden's acting and reproduced that quality in his criticism.

A beggar in the hands of Michael Angelo, says Fuseli, rose the Patriarch of Poverty. So the gusto of Munden antiquates and ennobles what it touches. His pots and his ladles are as grand and primal as the seething-pots and hooks seen in old prophetic vision. A tub of butter, contemplated by him, amounts to a Platonic idea. He understands a leg of mutton in its quiddity. He stands wondering, amid the common-place materials of life, like primaeval man with the sun and stars about him. (II, 149).

In the essays on Munden and Dodd Lamb's immense personal pleasure in their performances influenced his appreciation, and he produced a response which exploited the resources of his own mind in order to do justice to that of the actor. Lamb conveyed a full articulation of the impression which the acting had made upon him. In the essay on Dodd his description of Dodd's facial expressions dealt, as in the essay on Munden, with the vivid but not visual impression created.

In expressing slowness of apprehension this actor surpassed all others. You could see the first dawn of an idea stealing slowly over his countenance, climbing up by little and little, with a painful process, till it cleared up at last to the fulness of a twilight conception – its highest meridian. He seemed to keep back his intellect, as some have had the power to retard their pulsation. The balloon takes less time in filling, than it took to cover the expansion of his broad moony face over all its quarters with expression. A glimmer of understanding would appear in a corner of his eye, and for lack of fuel go out again. A part of his forehead would catch a little intelligence, and be a long time in communicating it to the remainder. (II, 136).

Imagery supplied the place of literal description. Lamb used references to light as an image of intellectual perception, in 'dawn' which suggested the slow appearance of an immature idea on a blank face, and in 'twilight' (as the point of the idea's fullest clarification) which conveyed the character's ultimate inability to develop the idea completely. The 'lack of fuel' implied a dull mind, without energy; all movement was lethargic and difficult; and the balloon's hollowness reflected the character's empty head. Lamb recreated Dodd's performance in order to capture for his readers the effect which that actor stimulated. But if Dodd was '*it,* as it came out of nature's hands', such acting did not come easily. Good comic acting did not just happen. It required a conscious effort of preparation and control on the part of the actor. 'Parsons and Dodd must have *thought* a good deal before they could have matured such exhibitions as their *Foresight* and *Aguecheek'* (I, 151). Lamb did not believe that improvisation should form the basis of the comic actor's art, but he rather advocated a careful and constant attention to their roles. This did not necessarily diminish the liveliness of a performance, for it did not demand the suppression of vitality. It urged a concentration based upon the knowledge of the effect which the actor sought.

Whereas Hazlitt was the greater critic of the theatre Lamb possessed the greater capacity for experiencing comic extravag-

ance of the kind presented by an actor like Munden. Hazlitt reacted for the most part very favourably to Munden but he had
some stringent reservations which differed from Lamb's judgements. If Munden had a weakness, it was that which Hazlitt
pointed to when he expressed a dislike for what he believed to
be Munden's conscious striving for effect and tendency to caricature. Hazlitt argued that 'if acting consisted in making wry faces,
he would be the greatest actor on the stage, instead of which he
is, on these occasions, only a bad clown' (V, 227). Leigh Hunt also
stressed this aspect of Munden's acting. He commented upon his
'two or three ludicrous gestures and an innumerable variety of
. . . fanciful contortions of countenance' and declared it an
'unnatural style of acting'.[13] The differences between Lamb and
Hazlitt were made clear in their reactions to Munden's playing of
the role of Johnny Gilpin. Lamb valued the performance very
little: 'In one only thing did I see him *act* – that is, support a
character; it was in a wretched farce called "Johnny Gilpin", for
Dowton's benefit' (I, 342). However, Hazlitt found gusto in this
performance, and after commenting upon the audience's
unfavourable reception of the play, he argued that Munden 'in
his part of a cockney' had produced a 'fine and inimitable piece
of acting' (XVIII, 223) which deserved praise from the audience.
Hazlitt acknowledged Munden's skill in comic extravagance but
he preferred the Munden of 'Johnny Gilpin'. Unlike Lamb, he
did not appreciate Munden when he found that, 'He is not only
perfectly conscious what he is about, but has a thorough understanding with the audience all along' (V, 226), but this suited
Lamb's distinction between the different degrees of stage illusion
required by tragedy and comedy, since in extravagant characters
in comedy an actor could succeed by maintaining a 'tacit understanding' (II, 163) with the audience.

iv

Lamb's critical essays on Fanny Kelly and Mrs Jordan contributed to the developing maturity of his ideas on the acting
techniques most suited to different kinds of drama. On 18 July
1813, when his first theatrical criticism on Fanny Kelly appeared

under the heading of 'Table Talk' in Leigh Hunt's *The Examiner,* he praised her for her 'judicious attention to her part, with little or no reference to the spectators' (I, 152). This quality, which he did not cease to respect in her acting, assumed an important influence in the formation of his later ideas. In this essay, which E. V. Lucas entitled 'The New Acting', Lamb developed an emphatic contrast between those contemporary actresses who seemed to set a fashion of facile tricks to draw the applause of the audience, and whom he called the 'Dalilahs of the stage', and Fanny Kelly who did not exploit these techniques. 'I am not sure that the absence of this fault in Miss Kelly, and her judicious attention to her part, with little or no reference to the spectators, is one cause why her varied excellencies, though they are beginning to be perceived, have yet found their way more slowly to the approbation of the public, than they have deserved' (I, 152). She maintained her integrity and refused to compromise with an audience in order to enhance her popularity. In a later sonnet, Lamb acknowledged his high regard for her genuine ability and behaviour.

> You are not, Kelly, of the common strain,
> That stoop their pride and female honour down
> To please that many-headed beast *the town,*
> And vend their lavish smiles and tricks for gain. (V, 40).

His feelings were powerfully engaged in this poem. He presented his respect for the independent spirit of Fanny Kelly which contrasted with his contempt for the lack of dignity and professional conscience shown by her rivals.

Lamb objected to a tendency among actors to adopt easy methods and a superficial approach to their art. The shortcomings of others highlighted for him the serious attitude and good sense of Fanny Kelly and recalled to his mind former actors like Parsons and Dodd who had studied their roles with care. But in his own age, Lamb claimed:

> We do not want capable actors, but their end is answered with less pains. The way is to get a kind of familiarity with the audience, to strike up a kind of personal friendship, to be 'hail fellow, well met', with them: those excellent comedians, Bannister and Dowton, who had least need of these arts, have not disdained to use them. (I, 151).

In 1813 he had perhaps not developed the conception of comic acting which he presented in the essay 'On the Artificial Comedy of the Last Century' for in that later essay he praised Bannister for the successful application of the very technique upon which he had apparently cast an unfavourable judgement in 1813. At the time of 'The New Acting' Lamb had perhaps not yet differentiated between the different styles of comic acting which suited different kinds of drama, and he had not yet clarified the context in which deliberately 'artificial' acting could be required.

In his discussions of Fanny Kelly and Mrs Jordan he appreciated the naturalness of their acting. In 1814 *The Examiner* printed some comments by Lamb on Mrs Jordan's acting.

> She has not an artificial tone. . . . When we say she never did or could play the *Fine Lady,* we mean it to her honour. Her mind is essentially above the thing. But if the term *Lady* implies anything of graceful or delicate in the highest sense of those female attributes, in that best sense it is due to her. She is one, not of Congreve's, or Sheridan's, but of Shakespeare's *Ladies.*[14]

Hazlitt also distinguished between the female characters of Shakespeare and of Congreve and Sheridan. In Millamant, Hazlitt argued, 'The springs of nature, passion, or imagination are but feebly touched. The impressions appealed to, and with masterly address, are habitual, external, and conventional advantages' (VI, 73–4), but Perdita and Rosalind differed because the 'interest we feel is in themselves; the admiration they excite is for themselves. They do not depend upon the drapery of circumstances. It is nature that "blazons herself" in them' (VI, 74). The awareness of such a distinction influenced Lamb's conception of the acting techniques required in the playing of such characters. In 1819 his discussion of Fanny Kelly appeared in *Felix Farley's Bristol Journal,* and as with Mrs Jordan, so Lamb turned to Fanny Kelly's advantage her limitations in 'what are called fine lady parts'. Since such parts demanded 'the entire repression of all genius and feeling' (I, 186) Fanny Kelly's and Mrs Jordan's failure in them became a distinguishing mark of their excellence. In examining the acting techniques which certain roles demanded of the two actresses he commented upon the relationship with the audience which these techniques established.

To sustain a part of this kind to the life, a performer must be haunted by a perpetual sub-reference: she must be always thinking of herself, and how she looks, and how she deports herself in the eyes of the spectators; whereas the delight of actresses of true feeling, and their chief power, is to elude the personal notice of an audience, to escape into their parts, and hide themselves under the hood of their assumed character. Their most graceful self-possession is in fact a self-forgetfulness; an oblivion alike of self and of spectators. (I, 186).

Fanny Kelly instinctively concentrated fully upon her role, and this acting technique ensured her success in tragic roles but hindered her in the 'fine lady parts' of artificial comedy which required a consciousness of the audience. Thus these actresses excelled in the performance of Shakespearean heroines like Viola and Helena but were unsuited to play the ladies created by Congreve and Sheridan. This idea foreshadowed the essays 'On the Artificial Comedy of the Last Century' and on 'Stage Illusion'.

Lamb's judgement on Fanny Kelly found consistent support in the writings of his contemporaries. Hazlitt wrote that, 'She is not good at child's play, at the *make-believe* fine-lady, or the *make-believe* waiting maid. Hers is *bona fide* downright acting, and she must have something to do, in order to do it properly' (XVIII, 354). And Leigh Hunt judged her 'an actress of great sensibility; and what is more, without that perverter of it, affectation'.[15] She had, in Lamb's opinion, a voice 'meant by nature to convey nothing but truth and goodness'; and she lacked the confidence to deliver epilogues well because she needed 'the modest veil of personation'. All of her critics praised her naturalness. She seemed without artifice. She possessed that rarest and most valued of skills, a 'wonderful force of imagination' (I, 185), and this enabled her to express the innermost thoughts and feelings of the character she acted. It was this projection of the inner self which most affected Lamb's sensibility and which evoked a deep sympathetic response. Thus he judged Fanny Kelly's acting, as he did Munden's and Mrs Jordan's, by the impressions which it stimulated. He rarely allowed himself to be occupied by the external characteristics of a performance, and his criticism scarcely examined physical details. In a letter to Barron Field in 1827 he disclaimed the ability to describe the external features of a subject – in this instance costumes: 'I have no eye for forms and fashions. I substitute analogies, and get rid of the phenomenon by slurring in for its impression.'[16] His criticism of Fanny Kelly and Mrs Jordan illustrated this. In the 1819 essay Lamb wrote of Fanny Kelly:

This latter lady's is the joy of a freed spirit, escaping from care, as a bird that has been limed; her smiles, if I may use the expression, seemed saved out of the fire, relics which a good and innocent heart had snatched up as most portable; her contents are visitors, not inmates: she can lay them by altogether; and when she does so, I am not sure that she is not greatest. She is, in truth, no ordinary tragedian. Her Yarico is the most intense piece of acting which I ever witnessed, the most heartrending spectacle. To see her leaning upon that wretched reed, her lover – the very exhibition of whose character would be a moral offence, but for her clinging and noble credulity – to see her lean upon that flint, and by the strong workings of passion imagine it a god – is one of the most afflicting lessons of the yearnings of the human heart and its and mistakes, that ever was read upon a stage. The whole performance is every where *African,* fervid, glowing. (I, 185–6).

When Leigh Hunt reprinted this essay in *The Examiner* of 7–8 February 1819 he added a preface of his own in which he paid tribute to Lamb's criticism. He claimed that Fanny Kelly 'had finer criticism written upon her than any performer that ever trode the stage'.

Lamb denied the possibility of an 'account' of Mrs Jordan's acting of 'the disguised story of her love for Orsino' as Viola in *Twelfth Night,* and did not mention gesture, movement, or physical appearance. His attention fastened upon the idea not the object.

It was no set speech, that she had foreseen, so as to weave it into an harmonious period, line necessarily following line, to make up the music – yet I have heard it so spoken, or rather *read,* not without its grace and beauty – but, when she had declared her sister's history to be a 'blank', and that she 'never told her love', there was a pause, as if the story had ended – and then the image of the 'worm in the bud' came up as a new suggestion – and the heightened image of 'Patience' still followed after that, as by some growing (and not mechanical) process, thought springing up after thought, I would almost say, as they were watered by her tears. So in those fine lines –

Write loyal cantos of condemned love –
Hollow your name to the reverberate hills –

there was no preparation made in the foregoing image for that which was to follow. (II, 132–3).

Lamb perhaps intended an implicit attack on Reynolds's version of the play which had recently been produced at Covent Garden, and in which Maria Tree 'played and sang Viola'.[17] He preferred the natural speaking voice for this role. The speech belonged to Mrs Jordan rather than existing apart from her as something which she had learnt and consciously prepared. She imposed no artificial form upon the language. She did not give the impression that she was reciting lines of poetry, and she respected the manner in which Shakespeare had integrated his imagery into the speech. Lamb revealed his own conception of the way in which Shakespeare's language should be delivered. He distinguished her presentation of her speech as 'growing (and not mechanical)', just as Coleridge believed that in Shakespeare 'all is growth, evolution, . . . each line, each word almost, begets the following – and the will of the writer is an interfusion, a continuous agency, no series of separate acts'.[18] Lamb valued the spontaneity of Mrs Jordan's acting. When she delivered her speech she did not simply repeat it but she created it. 'She used no rhetoric in her passion; or it was nature's own rhetoric, most legitimate then, when it seemed without rule or law' (II, 133). Lamb had an extreme dislike for formal organization. He dismissed Charron as 'a mere piece of formality, scholastic dry bones, without sinew or living flesh', but praised Montaigne because 'his own character pervades the whole, and binds it sweetly together' (I, 153). Much of Lamb's own spirit emanated in his comments on Fanny Kelly and Mrs Jordan. Indeed, the manner of their acting encouraged the emotional involvement, the identification of the spectator. This was diametrically opposed to the kind of acting which formed the centre of his discussion of 'artificial' acting in the essay 'On the Artificial Comedy of the Last Century'.

V.

The essay 'On the Artificial Comedy of the Last Century' is well known, often quoted, but rarely examined and understood in its context. Lamb did not confine his discussion to Restoration comedy but he included a good deal of comment on Sheridan's *The School for Scandal* and on contemporary drama. The ideas which he articulated derived not solely from a consideration of plays but also from his theories on acting. His ideas on acting and dramatic illusion which he stated in 'Stage Illusion', and which had developed as an integral part of his critical thinking on the theatre in the preceding years, determined his attitude towards artificial comedy. Lamb based this essay on his practical knowledge of theatrical performance and attempted to defend artificial comedy against the charge of immorality. Whereas he willingly accepted the imaginative experience which the theatre offered and did not require the facile satisfaction of a 'notional justice, notional beneficence' (II, 146), he considered his contemporary audiences only too prone to the false application of moral judgement in the theatre. He did not believe that questions of moral judgement arose in what he called artificial comedy, because he thought that the world of the plays was 'altogether a speculative scene of things, which has no reference whatever to the world that is', and that the characters 'in their own sphere, do not offend my moral sense; in fact they do not appeal to it at all' (II, 143).

Lamb's idea first developed in the essay 'On Some of the Old Actors' where it evolved directly from a consideration of the acting techniques of Bannister and Palmer. Unlike the natural acting which Lamb praised in Fanny Kelly and Mrs Jordan, Palmer and Bannister occasionally employed an artificial mode of acting. Of Palmer Lamb wrote:

Jack had two voices, – both plausible, hypocritical and insinuating; but his secondary or supplemental voice still more decisively histrionic than his common one. It was reserved for the spectator; and the dramatis personae were supposed to know nothing at all about it. The *lies* of young Wilding, and the *sentiments* in Joseph Surface, were thus marked out in a sort of italics to the audience. This secret correspondence with the company before the curtain (which is the bane and death of tragedy) has an extremely happy effect in some kinds of comedy, in the more highly artificial comedy of Congreve or of Sheridan especially, where the absolute sense of reality (so indispensable to scenes of interest) is not required, or would rather interfere to diminish your pleasure. (II, 140).

When Bannister played Ben, in *Love for Love,* and had to show in that character an 'insensibility which in real life would be revolting' (II, 140) he acted in such a manner as to create the impression of a 'delightful phantom – the creature dear to half-belief', and the result was that he did not 'wound the moral sense' of the spectator. An actor who played the part realistically, who made Ben into 'a downright concretion of a Wapping sailor – a jolly warm-hearted Jack tar' (II, 141), disturbed the spectator's moral sense.

Lamb developed this discussion in the essay 'On the Artificial Comedy of the Last Century'. Such comedy depicted the 'fictitious half-believed personages of the stage' (II, 142) in whose actions and feelings the audience's sympathies should not be fully engaged, and the actor had consequently to deliberately reduce the audience's emotional involvement, to create a psychological distance between them and the performance. Lamb's experience of the theatre had shown him that one way in which the actor could achieve this was by using two voices, as did Palmer in his acting of Joseph Surface: 'He was playing to you all the while that he was playing upon Sir Peter and his lady. You had the first intimation of a sentiment before it was upon his lips. His altered voice was meant to you, and you were to suppose that his fictitious co-flutterers on the stage perceived nothing at all of it' (II, 145). The result of Palmer's 'highly artificial manner' was that it 'counteracted every disagreeable impression which you might have received from the contrast, supposing them real, between the two brothers' (II, 145). Artificial acting took the character into 'the regions of pure comedy, where no cold moral reigns' (II, 145), and Lamb regretted that contemporary actors had abandoned the techniques of artificial acting: 'Sir Peter Teazle must be no longer the comic idea of a fretful old bachelor bridegroom, whose teasings (while King acted it) were evidently as much played off at you, as they were meant to concern any body on the stage, – he must be a real person' (II, 146).

At the same time as theatrical production changed characters like Joseph Surface into real people so it allowed the introduction of moral judgement. Lamb's argument implied that actors held much responsibility for this and could determine the nature of the audience's reaction; but, as he acknowledged, there were always spectators who insisted on maintaining moral judgement in the theatre. In *The Public Advertiser* of 1 December 1787 a reviewer asked: 'But without a moral tendency, what advantage can possibly be gained from visiting the theatre?' Lamb considered artificial comedy as an entertainment and reproached those who 'dare not contemplate an Atlantis, a scheme, out of which our coxcombical moral sense is for a little transitory ease excluded' (II, 144). The theatre offered freedom to the imagination rather than an obligation to live 'our toilsome lives twice over' (II, 142). He distinguished between those moral standards which controlled his response to real life and those which operated when he saw artificial comedy, whereas the majority of spectators could not change their attitudes with this flexibility when they entered a theatre. Lamb also made a crucial distinction between artificial comedy and modern 'drama of common life' and the former's unreality must be judged in comparison with the latter's reality. Lamb admitted that if one of the characters of artificial comedy appeared in 'a modern play' then 'my virtuous indignation shall rise against the profligate wretch as warmly as the Catos of the pit could desire; because in a modern play I am to judge of the right and the wrong' (II, 143). Thus, in a letter to Godwin he objected to one of Godwin's ideas for a proposed play because he found the idea immoral in a contemporary play: 'Is it the best sort of feeling? Is it a feeling to be exposed on theatres to mothers and daughters?' (*Letters*, I, 275). Moral references in contemporary plays called the spectator's judgement into action. The characters had 'got into a moral world' (II, 143).

Lamb argued that in artificial comedy the characters engaged in actions which would have involved unpleasant consequences in the kind of world inhabited by the audience but that no such consequences were 'produced in *their* world'. Lamb declared that 'No deep affections are disquieted, – no holy wedlock bands are snapped asunder, – for affections depth and wedded faith are not of the growth of that soil' (II, 144). If the audience, sustained by the impression created by the actor, could be lead to suppose that no moral laws were violated because none existed amongst the characters on the stage, then moral values could only exist in the theatrical response if the audience insisted on applying the moral standards of their everyday life. They allowed the interference of a moral frame of reference. Lamb judged only by the effect which the play created upon him in the theatre, and thus he bypassed consideration of whether the play in itself was immoral. He argued that if the audience adopted the necessary attitudes then they would not *think* the play immoral. He concentrated his argument on audience response. He lamented that amongst his contemporaries there were 'no such middle emotions as dramatic interests left' (II, 141), and his view that artificial comedy presented the 'fictitious half-believed personages' suggested that the mode of comic response peculiar to artificial comedy depended upon the double perspective produced by an audience's willingness to believe and by its simultaneous consciousness of the fiction. Thus in the mind of the spectator there ideally existed neither complete illusion nor a thoroughly detached judgement of the play's fictitiousness. Artificial acting could create this response.

Lamb believed that Congreve's plays benefitted from the exclusion of characters who would have contributed to the formation of a moral frame of reference *within the play*. Congreve

spread a privation of moral light, I will call it, rather than by the ugly name of palpable darkness, over his creations; and his shadows flit before you without distinction or preference. Had he introduced a good character, a single gush of moral feeling, a revulsion of the judgement to actual life and actual duties, the impertinent Goshen would have only lighted to the discovery of deformities, which now are none, because we think them none. (II, 143).

Congreve also presented characters who did not excite the audience's passions, and their coldness contributed to their moral anonymity: 'you neither hate nor love his personages – and I think it is owing to this very indifference for any, that you endure the whole' (II, 143). No emotional involvement existed. The 'fortunes of Othello and Desdemona' were not at stake in artificial comedy.

Macaulay objected ferociously to Lamb's argument: 'The morality of the *Country Wife* and the *Old Bachelor* is the morality, not, as Mr Charles Lamb maintains, of an unreal world, but of a world which is a great deal too real. It is the morality, not of a chaotic people, but of low town-rakes, and of those ladies whom the newspapers call "dashing Cyprians".'[19] Lamb knew perfectly well that Restoration society included characters as immoral as those of Wycherley and Congreve. In the essay 'On the Tragedies of Shakspeare' he wrote that 'doubtless without some vicious alloy, the impure ears of that age [Dryden's] would never have sate out to hear so much innocence of love as is contained in the sweet courtship of Ferdinand and Miranda' (I, 109). Houghton quoted Lamb's comment on Burnet's *History of His Own Times* as a work 'Full of scandal, which all true history is. No palliatives, but all the stark wickedness, that actually gives the *momentum* to national actors' (*Letters,* I, 176–7). Houghton suggested that Lamb knew that this applied to social as well as political life, and that he 'did not need Macaulay to tell him that Wycherley and Congreve wrote from observation'.[20] He knew that Congreve did not write in a vacuum, but he did not suppose that he simply recorded the vices of his age. Lamb understood as clearly as did Macaulay that vice existed in all periods, but he distinguished between art and history. He argued that the morality of artificial comedy became unreal when its appropriate artistic presentation (which was artificial acting) made it seem so.

Important critical objections to Lamb's essay have stressed that he divorced artificial comedy from what E. E. Stoll called its 'necessary ultimate relation to morality and life'.[21] Lamb suggested that artificial comedy created its own autonomous world and he arrived at this defence in reaction against the excesses of contemporary moral judgement of these plays. Contemporary audiences applied to the characters of artificial comedy the rigorous moral standards of their real lives. Lamb proposed that if artificial acting techniques maintained the 'fictitious half-believed personages of the stage' and kept the audience's emotions distant, then the audience were not required to condemn the morality of the plays; whereas if the plays were represented realistically moral judgements could interfere. The argument derived from practical experience of the theatre. When Palmer acted Joseph Surface he conveyed 'the downright *acted* villany of the part, so different from the pleasure of conscious actual wickedness, – the hypocritical assumption of hypocrisy', and consequently 'he divided the palm with me with his better brother' (II, 144). But the contemporary actor 'would instinctively avoid every turn which might tend to unrealise, and so to make the character fascinating. He must take his cue from his spectators, who would expect a bad man and a good man . . . rigidly opposed to each other' (II, 145). Lamb did not produce good criticism on Restoration comedy, but he did develop a sound analysis of audience reaction in the theatre and of the different effects which dissimilar acting techniques created on him.

V Lamb as Critic of Shakespeare

In his essay 'On the Tragedies of Shakspere, Considered with Reference to their Fitness for Stage Representation' Lamb argued that the plays of Shakespeare were 'less calculated for performance on a stage than those of almost any other dramatist whatever' (I, 99), and whilst he never contested Shakespeare's supreme greatness as a writer for the theatre and did not oppose stage presentations of his plays, he did express reservations about the theatrical possibilities of presenting those plays which were distinguished by the excellence of the dramatist's poetry and intellect. He acknowledged a radical difference between the text read in the study and the play performed in the theatre, and critics such as Johnson, Coleridge, Hazlitt, Bradley, and T. S. Eliot have shared this view. Boswell reported Johnson's remark that 'many of Shakespeare's plays are the worse for being acted'. Bradley wrote on the subject of the tragedies that 'as Lamb declared, theatrical representation gives only a part of what we imagine when we read them', and he claimed that in *King Lear* 'there is something in its very essence which is at war with the senses, and demands a purely imaginative realisation'. Eliot argued in his essay entitled 'Four Elizabethan Dramatists' that Shakespeare was a dramatist 'to be read rather than seen, because it is precisely in that drama which depends upon an actor of genius, that we ought to be on our guard against the actor'.[1]

Lamb insisted that he was 'not arguing that Hamlet should not be acted, but how much Hamlet is made another thing by being acted' (I, 101), and this generates a crucial question. Did Lamb suggest that the stage inevitably distorted Shakespeare's Hamlet because it lacked the possibility of representing him sufficiently well, or did he simply mean that contemporary productions alone made Hamlet into something different from Shakespeare's Hamlet? This latter argument followed many bad productions and went back at least to a very early theatre reviewer who wrote in *The Prompter* of 23 May 1735:

> Let him consider the Effect of a *Moving Scene,* on *Himself,* when He *reads* it, at Home; and *compare* it with the Effect of That very same Scene, when he *sees,* and *hears* it, on the *Stages* – He will remember, that the Passage which mov'd him, to the utmost Degree, in his *Closet,* gave him no Touch of *Emotion,* at the *Theatre:* where, yet, He will reflect, that, had it not been *un-naturally,* and *unknowingly,* represented, It must have *doubled* (instead of *losing*) its influence.

This critic remained confident that the difficulty concerned the manner of that particular production, but when Lamb encountered a similar experience he was less easily satisfied. In the essay on Shakespeare he articulated his views, and his argument suffered misinterpretation almost immediately. John Wilson, who reviewed Lamb's *Works* in *Blackwood's Edinburgh Magazine* for August 1818, expressed some of the criticisms which were to recur.

> Shakespeare gives us in his play all that is in the power of human actors to express, every variety of human passion that can be shewn by the voices, countenances, or bodies of men. If he gives us a great deal more than this, so much the better; but we are at a loss to conceive why that should make his plays worse fitted for representation. We agree with Mr Lamb, that Shakespeare's plays read better in the closet than those of any other writer, and this is all that his argument seems to us to prove: we cannot see, that merely because they read better in the closet, they should *therefore* act the worse on the stage.[2]

Lamb did not write 'worse fitted' but 'less calculated' and in the context the two phrases were not identical in meaning. Lamb's exact words were:

> It may seem a paradox, but I cannot help being of opinion that the plays of Shakspeare are less calculated for performance on a stage, than those of almost any other dramatist whatever. Their distinguished excellence is a reason that they should be so. There is so much in them, which comes not under the province of acting, with which eye, and tone, and gesture, have nothing to do. (I, 99).

Wilson distorted Lamb's meaning. He neglected the comparative nature of that part of Lamb's statement which dealt with theatrical representation, for Lamb here judged Shakespeare in relation to other dramatists. Further, Wilson falsely attributed to Lamb the suggestion that the richness of Shakespeare's plays made them 'worse fitted for representation'. Lamb neither condemned nor praised the quality of Shakespeare's plays in his phrase 'less calculated . . . than' but rather defined their nature. Wilson implied that Lamb depreciated the value of Shakespeare's plays in the theatre, but a careful reading of Lamb's text refutes this idea. Wilson appreciated Lamb's suggestion that Shakespeare had provided more in his play than a stage performance could adequately present, but he failed to suspect that this was probably the very reason why Lamb chose a word like 'calculated' rather than a word like suited or fitted. As Lamb understood it, a play calculated for the stage exploited those effects which were most likely to succeed in the theatre. He used the word 'calculated' in this way when he commented upon Garrick's delivery of some interpolated speeches in *Richard III:* 'Yet I doubt not he delivered this vulgar stuff with as much anxiety of emphasis as any of the genuine parts; and for acting, it is as well calculated as any' (I, 105). Lamb's critical judgement regarded the speeches as 'vulgar stuff' but despite that he had to acknowledge that they were 'as well calculated' for acting on stage. Here, as in the earlier comment, the word 'calculated' did not relate to the quality of the writing but to the likely effect which the writing could evoke in the theatre. Lamb argued that Shakespeare did not compose his plays with as exclusive an attention to theatrical effect as displayed by some other dramatists or by men like Garrick who altered Shakespeare's plays to increase their theatrical effectiveness. The enormous success of Garrick's alterations of plays like, for example, *Romeo and Juliet* conclusively showed that a Shakespearean play could be more effective on the stage if adapted. Fanny Kemble acknowledged against her better judgement that Garrick knew perfectly well what he was doing: 'all the frantic rushing and tortured writhing and uproar of noisy anguish of the usual stage ending seemed utter desecration to me; but Garrick was an actor, the first of actors, and his death-scene of the lovers and ending of the play is much more theatrically effective than Shakespeare'.[3] For Lamb the major distinguishing qualities of Shakespeare's plays were 'poetry' and 'stupendous intellect' and he argued that these qualities did not necessarily produce the most effective theatrical writing. The word 'calculated' also seemed to raise the question of Shakespeare's intentions, but Lamb did not develop this. He knew as well as Coleridge that Elizabethan theatrical production differed from that of his contemporary theatre, but he did not consider the possibility that Shakespeare could have written for audiences who reacted very differently from those of the eighteenth and nineteenth centuries. Such a possibility bears upon the applicability of 'calculated'.

In order to assess the degree to which Lamb's comments on the impossibility of acting Shakespeare were an absolute judgement on the plays and not simply a denigration of the productions which he witnessed, his essays on art provide valuable help. Lamb applied similar principles both in his criticism of the theatre and of painting and the essays 'On the Genius and Character of Hogarth' and the 'Barrenness of the Imaginative Faculty in the Productions of Modern Art' can clarify his concern with the aesthetic issue of the potential of a stage performance of poetic drama. He developed distinctions between meditation and observation and between poetic and pictorial subjects, and this directed his attention to the qualities of mind embodied in a work of art whether it was a play or a painting. The criticism of painting suggests that the essay on Shakespeare stemmed not only from Lamb's reaction to contemporary theatrical production but also from his concern with an aesthetic issue. The essay on Hogarth which was printed in *The Reflector,* no. 3 (1811) preceded the essay on Shakespeare (*The Reflector,* no. 4) by three months, and Lamb appreciated both Hogarth's works as well as Shakespeare's plays as 'objects of meditation' (I, 106). Just as Shakespeare 'transfused his own poetical character into the persons of his drama' so in Hogarth the 'reflection of the artist's own intellect from the faces of his characters, is one reason why the works of Hogarth, so much more than those of any other artist are objects of meditation. Our intellectual natures love the mirror which gives them back their own likenesses. The mental eye will not bend long with delight upon vacancy' (I, 78). This concern with the artist's intellect formed the basis of Lamb's initial reaction to the Garrick monument in Westminster Abbey, which had compared the actor and poet and provoked the essay on Shakespeare. The sonnet on Garrick's monument infuriated Lamb by suggesting that 'Shakspeare and Garrick like twin-stars shall shine'. Lamb maintained that an enormous difference existed between the qualities of mind necessary to a poet and to an actor. The poet required an 'absolute mastery over the heart and soul of man' (I, 97) and needed to 'know the internal workings and movements of a great mind . . . the *when* and the *why* and the *how far* they should be moved' (I, 98), whereas the actor employed external movements like gesture and facial expression in order to communicate the meaning to the audience by evoking in them the necessary effect. People should not 'confound the power of originating poetical images and conceptions with the faculty of being able to read or recite the same when put into words' (I, 97). ·

The best artist did not reproduce what he simply observed but invested his subject with a vision peculiar to his own mind, and Shakespeare demonstrated this capacity more clearly than anyone:

> We talk of Shakespeare's admirable observation of life, when we should feel, that not from a petty inquisition into those cheap and every-day characters which surrounded him, as they surround us, but from his own mind, which was, to borrow a phrase of Ben Jonson's, the very 'sphere of humanity', he fetched those images of virtue and of knowledge, of which every one of us recognizing a part, think we comprehend in our natures the whole. (I, 102–3).

Lamb's criticism distinguished between observation and meditation. Coleridge also argued that 'Shakespeare's characters are all *genera* intensely individualized; the results of meditation, of which observation supplied the drapery and the colours necessary to combine them with each other'.[4] He regarded observation as a passive activity whereas in meditation the mind was active. The idea of a work came not from observation but from the poet's mind:

> It has escaped some critics, that in the Fine Arts the Mental Initiative must necessarily proceed from within. Hence we find them giving, as it were, recipes to form a Poet, by placing him in certain directions and positions; as if they thought that every deer-stealer might, if he pleased become a Shakespeare, or that Shakespeare's mind was made up of the shreds and patches of the books of his day, which by good fortune he happened to read in such an order that they successively fitted into the scenes of *Macbeth, Othello, The Tempest, As You Like It*.[5]

This shows why Coleridge emphasized the importance of subjectivity in the creative experience. The same critical thinking informed his distinction between copy and imitation. He likened copy to a passive reproduction of what the eye had seen, whereas imitation required the mental activity of meditation.[6] Lamb, Hazlitt, and Coleridge all opposed the emphasis on the external features of a subject, and for them the aesthetic experience was not primarily based upon visual appreciation. Hazlitt insisted that 'objects of sense are not as it were simple and self-evident propositions, but admit of endless analysis and the most subtle investigation. We do not see nature with our eyes, but with our understandings and our hearts. To suppose that we see the whole of any object, merely by looking at it, is a vulgar error' (XX, 388). Hazlitt here argued that the aesthetic experience, if not merely sensory, was not solely intellectual either. Lamb too believed that the heart and feelings played an important role. He wanted figures with life and feeling, not 'furniture-faces' (I, 84), and admired Hogarth's ability to do this even with material objects: 'the dumb rhetoric of the scenery – for tables, and chairs, and joint-stools in Hogarth, are living and significant things' (I, 85).

Lamb stressed that the mental activity of the spectator always influenced his response: 'In the perusal of a book, or of a picture, much of the impression which we receive depends upon the habit of mind which we bring with us to such perusal' (I, 72). He applied this idea in his essay 'On the Artificial Comedy of the Last Century' where he criticized audiences who refused to adapt their approach to the necessary requirements made by the play. The response to painting depended upon the ability to think and feel, but many people could only respond to the external features of a work to which they applied superficial and meaningless labels:

> We are for ever deceiving ourselves with names and theories. We call one man a great historical painter, because he has taken for his subjects kings or great men, or transactions over which time has thrown a grandeur. We term another the painter of common life, and set him down in our minds for an artist of an inferior class, without reflecting whether the quantity of thought shewn by the latter may not much more than level the distinction which their mere choice of subjects may seem to place between them; or whether, in fact, from

that very common life a great artist may not extract as deep an interest as another man from that which we are pleased to call history. (I, 74–5).

Lamb also stated his strong opposition to 'the extreme narrowness of system . . . that rage for classification' (I, 74) since he believed that it was this kind of thinking which could produce judgement by externals.

Merely visual responses could not provide an accurate judgement of an artist's imagination, that faculty which he held in the highest esteem. He acknowledged the shaping and unifying power of the imagination 'which draws all things to one, – which makes things animate and inanimate, beings with their attributes, subjects and their accessories, take one colour, and serve to one effect' (I, 73). In the essay on the 'Barrenness of the Imaginative Faculty in the Productions of Modern Art' he expressed at more length what he understood by the ability to treat a story imaginatively.

By this we mean, upon whom his subject has so acted, that it has seemed to direct *him* – not to be arranged by him? Any upon whom its leading or collateral points have impressed themselves so tyrannically, that he dared not treat it otherwise, lest he should falsify a revelation? And that has imparted to his compositions, not merely so much truth as is enough to convey a story with clearness, but that individualising property, which should keep the subject so treated distinct in feature from every other subject, however similar, and to common apprehensions almost identical; so as that we might say, this and this part could have found an appropriate place in no other picture in the world but this? (II, 226).

Two main points emerge. Firstly, Lamb, like Coleridge, strongly affirmed the subjective element in artistic creation, for the experience represented in the painting was the artist's intensely personal way of looking at his subject. An artist with imagination could not tamper with this impression and of necessity surrendered any desire to distort or re-arrange his subject. This idea related closely to the concept of sympathetic identification. S. M. Tave pointed out the role of such eighteenth-century Scottish philosophers as Hume and Adam Smith in the developing emphasis on sympathy as 'an essential force in both ethical action and aesthetic creation',[7] and it strongly influenced the Romantic writers. The will of the artist seemed controlled by his subject because of the very close interaction between artist and subject. All of the parts of the work belonged exactly where they appeared and none could be altered without destroying the work. They all contributed to the organic unity of the whole. Secondly, Lamb suggested that the imagination produced imitation and not copy. The truth of a work of art did not depend solely upon its relation to an objective reality, and Lamb elucidated this a little later in the essay: 'By a wise falsification, the great masters of painting got at their true conclusions; by not showing the actual appearances, that is, all that was to be seen at any given moment by an indifferent eye, but only what the eye might be supposed to see in the doing or suffering of some portentous action' (II, 230). The 'stupendous genius' of artists like Leonardo da Vinci found that truth consisted in the artist's fidelity to his thoughts and feelings, and not to physical appearances. Lamb praised da Vinci's 'wonderful personification of the Logos or third person of the Trinity, grasping a globe . . . where the hand was by the boldest licence twice as big as the truth of drawing warranted, yet the effect to every one that saw it, by some magic of genius, was confessed to be not *monstrous,* but *miraculous* and *silencing.* It could not be gainsaid' (I, 151). Again, Coleridge advocated the same principle:

> a moment's reflection suffices to make every man conscious of what every man must have before felt, that the drama is an *imitation* of reality, not a *copy* – and that imitation is contra-distinguished from copy by this: that a certain quantum of difference is essential to the former, and an indispensable condition and cause of the pleasure we derive from it; while in a copy it is a defect, contravening its name and purpose. (*SC,* I, 127–8).

He applied this principle to actors as well, and argued that they should not be 'a mere *Copy,* a *facsimile,* but an *imitation,* of Nature. . . . A good actor is Pygmalion's Statue, a work of exquisite *art, animated* & gifted with *motion;* but still *art,* still a species of *Poetry'.*[8] The quality of the difference between copy and imitation distinguished the imaginative artist. Lamb suggested that the eye of the best artist was never 'indifferent', it involved itself with the subject, imparted its own personality, and, therefore, in order to embody truthfully its unique vision, 'Not all that

is optically possible to be seen, is to be shown in every picture'
(II, 230).

Because Lamb did not base his aesthetic judgement of painting
upon its appeal to the eyes, he realized that he could not accept
much of the work of his contemporaries. His principle of
criticism applied to Shakespeare's characters as well as to
painting:

> Artists again err in the confounding of *poetic* with *pictorial*
> *subjects.* In the latter, the exterior accidents are nearly every-
> thing, the unseen qualities as nothing. Othello's colour – the
> infirmities and corpulence of a Sir John Falstaff – do they
> haunt us perpetually in the reading? or are they obtruded upon
> our conceptions one time for ninety-nine that we are lost in
> admiration at the respective moral or intellectual attributes of
> the character? But in a picture Othello is *always* a Blackamoor;
> and the other only Plump Jack. (II, 233).

Pictures of Shakespearean characters restricted Lamb's imagination. In a letter to Samuel Rogers in December 1833 he wrote:

> What injury (short of the theatres) did not Boydell's
> 'Shakespeare Gallery' do me with Shakespeare? – to have
> Opie's Shakespeare, Northcote's Shakespeare, light-headed
> Fuseli's Shakespeare, heavy-headed Romney's Shakespeare,
> wooden-headed West's Shakespeare (though he did the best
> in 'Lear'), deaf-headed Reynolds's Shakespeare, instead of my,
> and everybody's Shakespeare. To be tied down to an authentic
> face of Juliet! To have Imogen's portrait! To confine the
> illimitable! (*Letters,* III, 394).

To Lamb Shakespeare's characters were poetic and not pictorial
subjects, and he did not think that their unseen qualities could be
defined objectively in a picture. The picture interfered with his
individual imaginative appreciation of the character. Lamb,
Hazlitt, and Coleridge rejected the eighteenth-century adherence
to the 'ut pictura poesis' theory, and when the theatre emphasized
scenery and the physical characteristics rather than the 'moral
or intellectual attributes of the character' it provoked these men
to their distinction between reading Shakespeare and seeing his
plays performed on stage. Lamb and Coleridge both regarded
Shakespeare's characters as the presentation of an idea, and an
idea came from the meditation and not the observation of the
poet. This generated a problem since in the theatre 'instead of

realizing an idea, we have only materialized and brought down a fine vision to the standard of flesh and blood. We have let go a dream, in quest of an unattainable substance' (I, 98). Lamb, and those who agreed with him, could not reconcile what seemed to them opposite interests. The play when read appealed primarily to the mind through its poetic language, whilst the play on the stage appealed primarily to the eye and shifted the emphasis away from the abstract appreciation of the ideas. Lamb did not advocate either reading or stage performance to the exclusion of the other, but argued essentially that a difference existed between the two. His essay had a basis in his critical theory.

ii

In the late eighteenth and early nineteenth centuries interpolated scenes, speeches, and characters often appeared in those plays of Shakespeare which were produced on the London Stage, with the result that those versions differed very substantially from Shakespeare's original texts. Garrick altered Shakespeare's plays as he pleased and introduced whatever new characters, speeches, or amendments to the plot that he thought necessary in order to suit his productions to the tastes of the age in which he lived. He maintained Tate's version of *King Lear,* with some amendments of his own, and so continued a tradition which was to keep the original off the stage until almost the middle of the nineteenth century. When Lamb wrote his essay on Shakespeare in 1811 he could never have seen *King Lear* performed in the original version, and he expressed his anger at the way in which Shakespeare's plays had been altered.

I am almost disposed to deny to Garrick the merit of being an admirer of Shakspeare. A true lover of his excellencies he certainly was not; for would any true lover of them have admitted into his matchless scenes such ribald trash as Tate and Cibber, and the rest of them, that

With their darkness durst affront his light,

have foisted into the acting plays of Shakspeare? (I, 105).
Lamb further attacked Shakespeare's alterers in a letter which he contributed to the *Spectator* in 1828. 'Sir, – Partaking in your

indignation at the sickly stuff interpolated by Tate in the genuine play of *King Lear,* I beg to lay before you certain kindred enormities that you may be less aware of' (I, 321). In the comments which followed Lamb criticized Tate's *Coriolanus,* Shadwell's *Timon of Athens,* and the 1678 acting edition of *Macbeth.*

The success of corrupt acting versions turned Lamb's wrath against audiences, so that in addition to his contempt for the arrogance of Shakespeare's alterers, he had scant respect for a public who could be so grossly deceived. With reference to the version of *Macbeth* which Betterton had acted at the beginning of the eighteenth century, he expressed stern disapproval of what 'our ancestors at that time were willing to accept for Shakspeare' I, 322), with the clear irony that the audiences of the nineteenth century still accepted something very similar. But Lamb's criticisms extended beyond a mere disapproval of individual audiences to a wider appraisal of *any* audience's critical abilities. His comments upon 'common auditors' referred to the audiences of any period, and he did not think them capable of appreciating the subtler skills of a dramatist as great as Shakespeare.

But of the grounds of the passion, its correspondence to a great or heroic nature, which is the only worthy object of tragedy, – that common auditors know any thing of this, or can have any such notions dinned into them by the mere strength of an actor's lungs, – that apprehensions foreign to them should be thus infused into them by storm, I can neither believe, nor understand how it can be possible. (I, 102).

Audiences demanded and enjoyed an exaggerated emphasis on visual effects, and the theatrical managements devoted much attention to novel and spectacular displays of scenery and costume. In Lamb's opinion such productions vulgarly distorted Shakespearean drama. They wasted energy on trivial and super-fluous details, and by drawing so much attention to those things they obstructed the audience's appreciation of essentials. Thus Lamb argued:

When Hamlet compares the two pictures of Gertrude's first and second husband, who wants to see the pictures? But in the acting, a miniature must be lugged out; which we know not to be the picture, but only to shew how finely a miniature may be represented. This shewing of every thing, levels all things: it makes tricks, bows, and curtesies, of importance. I, 111).

107

He attacked Garrick and his followers because he felt them to be the 'showmen of the scene' (I, 107). The harsh reactions of Lamb, Hazlitt, and Coleridge partially stemmed from their awareness that in Shakespeare's own time the stage productions had been of a very different kind. Coleridge wrote:

The theatre itself had no artificial, extraneous inducements – few scenes, little music – all that was to excite the senses in a high degree was wanting. Shakespeare himself said: 'We appeal to your imaginations'. . . .

The circumstances of acting were altogether different from ours; it was much more of recitation, or rather a medium between recitation and what we now call recitation. The idea of the poet was always present, not of the actors, not of the things to be represented. It was at that time more a delight and employment for the intellect, than amusement for the senses. (*SC,* II, 85).

Bad productions and corrupt texts did not alone provoke these judgements.

For Lamb Shakespeare's major distinguishing qualities were his 'poetry' and his 'stupendous intellect' and he implied that the theatre sometimes hindered the fullest expression of such qualities. It could not faithfully convey the language and atmosphere of certain situations.

The love-dialogues of Romeo and Juliet, those silver-sweet sounds of lovers' tongues by night; the more intimate and sacred sweetness of nuptial colloquy between an Othello or a Posthumus with their married wives, all those delicacies which are so delightful in the reading . . . by the inherent fault of stage representation, how are these things sullied and turned from their very nature by being exposed to a large assembly. (I, 100).

He exempted actors from responsibility for this fault, for the actor 'must pronounce them *ore rotundo,* he must accompany them with his eye, he must insinuate them into his auditory by some trick of eye, tone, or gesture, or he fails. *He must be thinking all the while of his appearance, because he knows that all the while the spectators are judging of it'.* (I, 100–1). Theatre and audience constrained the actors to act as they did. The fault was an 'inherent fault of stage representation' and when Lamb chose the word 'inherent' he referred not to the particular inadequacies of any individual performance or performer but to a permanent fault which the theatre could never overcome or elude. The inability of the theatre to realize the poetry and atmosphere of, for instance, the 'love-dialogues of Romeo and Juliet' derived from an inherent fault, a fault integral to the medium of the theatre. Hazlitt later argued that: 'Poetry and the stage do not agree together. The attempt to reconcile them fails not only of effect but of decorum. The *ideal* has no place upon the stage, the imagination cannot sufficiently qualify the impressions of the senses'. (V, 234). Both Lamb and Hazlitt acknowledged a fundamental limitation of the theatre. These were absolute judgements on the theatrical possibilities of presenting Shakespearean tragedy and they did not depend solely upon responses to contemporary productions.

The critical judgements of Coleridge reinforced this opposition between the ideal and the senses. With reference to *The Tempest* Coleridge wrote:

It addresses itself entirely to the imaginative faculty; and although the illusion may be assisted by the effect on the senses of the complicated scenery and decorations of modern times yet this sort of assistance is dangerous. For the principal and only genuine excitement ought to come from within, – from the moved and sympathetic imagination; whereas, where so much is addressed to the more external senses of seeing and hearing, the spiritual vision is apt to languish, and the attraction from without will withdraw the mind from the proper and only legitimate interest which is intended to spring from within. (*SC,* I, 131–2).

The play had something 'almost miraculous' about it and could be best understood by the imagination. Coleridge saw a fundamental incongruity in the attempt to embellish the visual effects of a stage performance. The essence of the play consisted in its 'spiritual vision', and the stage's emphasis upon physical visual effects exaggerated the difference between Coleridge's ideal conception of the play's essential qualities and the response of his senses to a stage performance. Lamb argued that the reading of a Shakespearean tragedy 'presents to the fancy just so much of external appearances as to make us feel that we are among flesh and blood, while by far the greater and better part of our imagination is employed upon the thoughts and internal machinery of the character' (I, 111). He preferred a situation where the awareness of external appearances remained subservient to the functioning of the imaginative response. His own criticism showed this concern, but many theatrical reviewers only reflected in their comments an interest in external details. Lamb objected to those who valued, for example, Mrs Siddons's manner of dismissing the guests in the Banquet scene in *Macbeth,* and who praised her 'Mrs Beverley in the same way as . . . [her] Lady Macbeth' (I, 104). He did not consider Garrick's fame in *Hamlet* to be well supported by the kind of argument presented by his commentators: 'Those who tell me of him, speak of his eye, of the magic of his eye, and of his commanding voice: physical properties, vastly desirable in an actor, and without which he can never insinuate meaning into an auditory, – but what have they to do with Hamlet? what have they to do with intellect?' (I, 101). This highlighted the different approach which existed in Lamb's theatrical criticism.

For Lamb the critical interest of a Shakespearean character centred on that character's inner being. Hamlet's 'moral sense' and 'silent meditations' most occupied Lamb's thoughts. He suggested that most of the action involving Hamlet took place within the man himself.

> Why, nine parts in ten of what Hamlet does, are transactions between himself and his moral sense, they are the effusions of his solitary musings, which he retires to holes and corners and the most sequestered parts of the palace to pour forth; or rather, they are the silent meditations with which his bosom is bursting, reduced to *words* for the sake of the reader, who must else remain ignorant of what is passing there. (I, 100).

As Hamlet declared, he had 'that within which passes show' (I. ii. 85). Similarly, Lamb's fascination with Othello derived from 'the texture of Othello's mind, the inward construction marvellously laid open with all its strengths and weaknesses, its heroic confidences and its human misgivings, its agonies of hate springing from the depths of love' (I, 102). His problem with the theatre stemmed from the dichotomy which existed between his own desire to probe the psychology of the created character, in search of the 'motives and grounds of the passion' (I, 98), and the theatre's emphasis on an appeal to the senses. His experience of theatrical production confirmed his belief that audiences responded favourably to the broadest theatrical effects: 'the more coarse and palpable the passion is, the more hold upon the eyes and ears of the spectators the performer obviously possesses. For this reason, scolding scenes, scenes where two persons talk themselves into a fit of fury, and then in a surprising manner talk themselves out of it again, have always been the most popular upon our stage' (I, 99). He believed that the stage hindered his perception of the individual subtleties of Shakespearean tragic heroes. By attention to the 'impulses' rather than the 'acts' (I, 106) of the character he could distinguish between Richard III, Iago, and Macbeth. They were unique creations, and that could be perceived not by differentiating their actions but by studying their meditations. An emphasis on their actions rather than their minds blurred their distinctive qualities. It reduced characters like a Macbeth or an Othello to the level of a George Barnwell, and led audiences to make superficial judgements. They might believe a 'rope more due to Othello than to Barnwell' (I, 102).

Lamb did not concern himself with the morality of the deeds of men like Richard, Iago, or Macbeth but rather with their 'ambition, the aspiring spirit, the intellectual activity, which prompts them to overleap those moral fences' (I, 106). As in his essay 'On the Artificial Comedy of the Last Century' so here he did not apply the moral standards of life. Unlike those eighteenth-century critics who argued, for example, that Hamlet taught that 'murder cannot lie hid',[9] Lamb resisted facile moral judgement. In the following comment on Hamlet the repeated use of *we* developed his irony:

> for the character itself, we find it in a play, and therefore we judge it a fit subject of dramatic representation. The play itself abounds in maxims and reflexions beyond any other, and therefore we consider it as a proper vehicle for conveying moral instruction. But Hamlet himself – what does he suffer meanwhile by being dragged forth as a public schoolmaster, to give lectures to the crowd! (I, 100).

Shakespeare did not preach, and Lamb refused to attribute to him the desire to communicate a simple moral which could be succinctly expressed in a catch-phrase.

Lamb did not conceive the nature of a major Shakespearean villain as something which could be summed up in a few brief, simple sentences. He considered Iago as a 'consummate villain' and not as one of the 'green probationers in mischief' (II, 134), just as Coleridge saw him not as a 'fellow with a countenance predestined for the gallows', but as 'an accomplished and artful villain' (*SC,* II, 277). Lamb suggested that if Richard had made a blatant demonstration of his wickedness then he would have deceived no-one. Not an easy man to fathom since full of 'that silent confidence, and steady self-command of the *experienced politician'* (I, 37), Richard was not a monster but rather an extremely complex human being. Thus Lamb found many qualities in him which countered our distaste at his villainy. He referred, in a letter to Robert Lloyd of 26 June 1801, to the

> most exquisite address to the Widowed Queen to court her daughter for him – the topics of maternal feeling, of a deep knowledge of the heart, are such as no monster could have supplied. Richard must have *felt* before he could feign so well; tho' ambition choked the good seed. I think it the most finished piece of Eloquence in the world.

But even if Shakespeare 'set out to paint a *monster* . . . his human sympathies produced a *man'* (*Letters,* I, 260), and in that judgement Lamb assumed the subjectivity of the creative process and implied that Shakespeare's characters reflected the author's consciousness, although, as he later pointed out in a note to the *Extracts from the Garrick Plays,* Shakespeare's sympathies, in contrast to those of Heywood, remained 'subordinate to poetry' (IV, 419).

Lamb elsewhere argued that Shakespeare drew upon his own imagination for his characters and not upon the physical world, and this remained consistent with the implication that total objectivity was not possible for him. When Lamb wrote that the 'Lear of Shakspeare cannot be acted' (I, 107) he referred to that character as an ideal conception of the poet's imagination. Lear was indissolubly linked with Shakespeare's mind. Only a reader with the deepest imaginative sympathy could approach such creations, but that was precisely what Coleridge, Lamb, and Hazlitt believed that they could achieve in reading. Lamb claimed that in the reading 'we see not Lear, but we are Lear, – we are in his mind' (I, 107), and Hazlitt wrote of Hamlet's speeches that 'their reality is in the reader's mind. It is *we* who are Hamlet' (IV, 232). But in the theatre the actor turned the character into a physical reality which prevented such a response. In Lamb's experience

112

Kemble's performance of Macbeth provoked a 'painful anxiety' whereas in the reading of the play 'the deed doing never presses upon us with the painful sense of presence' (I, 106). And the sight of Lear 'tottering about the stage with a walking-stick, turned out of doors by his daughters in a rainy night, has nothing in it but what is painful and disgusting' (I, 107). The 'sublime emotion' (I, 106) felt by a reader became vulgarized for the spectator in the theatre. Moreover, Coleridge argued that 'Mrs Siddons as Lady, and Kemble as Macbeth . . . might be the Macbeths of the Kembles, but they were not the Macbeths of Shakespeare' (*SC,* II, 278). For Lamb the actor's physical presence weighed the more heavily on his mind the better he knew the actor. 'It is difficult for a frequent playgoer to disembarass the idea of Hamlet from the person and voice of Mr K. We speak of Lady Macbeth, while we are in reality thinking of Mrs S' (I, 98). On stage person and voice came over too strongly and impeded the spectator's response to the idea of the character. The actor's interpretation prevented the spectator from attaining the closest imaginative contact with Shakespeare's creation.

Lamb, Hazlitt, and Coleridge developed ideal conceptions of Shakespearean plays which were based upon their reading of those plays. Thus Lamb had ideas about *Richard III* which contrasted with those of George Frederick Cooke, one of the leading actors of the role during Lamb's lifetime. Cooke portrayed Richard as a monster because he failed to communicate such aspects of Richard's character as 'the rich intellect which he displays, his resources, his wit, his buoyant spirits, his vast knowledge and insight into characters, the poetry of his part' (I, 106). He failed to match Lamb's conception of Richard. Cooke interpolated lines from other Shakespearean plays, when such lines were 'suitable to his manner of playing the part'.[10] This contradicted Lamb's requirements that an actor show 'his taste, by adhering, as much as possible, to the spirit and intention of the original Author, and to consult his *safety* in *steering* by the *Light,* which Shakespeare holds out to him, as by a great *Leading Star*' (I, 37). In reading the play Lamb reacted with sensitivity to Richard's poetry, but after seeing Cooke on stage he accused him of destroying the effect of Shakespeare's poetic language: 'the lofty imagery and high sentiments and high passions of *Poetry* come black and prose-smoked from his prose Lips' (*Letters,* I, 259). It seems that

113

contemporary productions rarely allowed poetry to exercise its power. Lamb recalled a blind man at a performance of *Richard III* at Drury Lane whose emotions responded so deeply to the language which he heard spoken on stage that tears came to his eyes. But this effect was nullified for the audience who could see because of the manner of the performance. The audience were reduced to laughing 'partly at him, and partly at the grotesque figures and wretched action of the women, who had been selected by managerial taste to personate those royal mourners' (I, 158). Lamb's response to the character of Richard was essentially based upon 'the poetry of the part' and that response could not be rekindled by an actor or a performance which relegated the poetry to a subordinate position.

Lamb remained conscious of the difficulties which stage presentations of complex characters involved, but he implied that the failings of many of his contemporaries were needlessly gross. He complained of the way in which, in Hamlet's scenes with Polonius and Ophelia, actors exploited the broadest theatrical effects and thus distorted Shakespeare's ideas. They made Hamlet 'shew contempt, and curl up the nose at Ophelia's father, – contempt in its very grossest and most hateful form; but they get applause by it: it is natural, people say; that is, the words are scornful, and the actor expresses scorn, and that they can judge of: but why so much scorn, and of that sort, they never think of asking' (I, 103). Lamb's comments severely denounced the superficial judgement of both actor and audience. Facile display brought success for an actor, so that many fell to the temptation of appealing to the least perceptive spectators. In his advice to the Players Hamlet acknowledged the ease with which 'unskilful' spectators could be pleased, but warned the Players to value the opinion of one 'judicious' spectator more highly than that of a 'whole theatre of others' (III. ii. 27–8). Lamb objected to actors who presented a character in one scene without reference to that character as he appeared in the rest of the play. He argued that contemporary productions failed to probe the nature and reason for Hamlet's scorn and that they thus neglected the crucial consideration.

Lamb's *Specimens* have encouraged the belief that he appreciated individual scenes rather than whole plays, and he himself professed an inability to 'grasp at a whole' (*Letters,* I, 362), but

114

he did not always sever his judgement of individual scenes from his response to the complete play. His comments on Hamlet's treatment of Polonius and Ophelia illustrate this. Lamb's total reaction to Hamlet included a recognition of 'gentility' in the character and he refused to judge Hamlet's abuse of Polonius and Ophelia in isolation from his general attitude. Lamb argued that Hamlet's actions were 'what we *forgive afterwards,* and explain by the whole of his character, but *at the time* they are harsh and unpleasant' (I, 103). In his criticism of Shakespeare he showed an awareness of the principle of the organic unity of a work of art, a principle which formed so vital a part of Coleridge's critical thinking. This principle produced an approach to form quite contrary to the earlier eighteenth-century neo-classical adherence to the unities. Coleridge distinguished between 'mechanic' and 'organic' form: 'The form is mechanic when on any given material we impress a pre-determined form, not necessarily arising out of the properties of the material . . . organic form, on the other hand, is innate; it shapes as it develops itself from within, and the fulness of its development is one and the same with the perfection of its outward form' (*SC,* I, 224). Shakespeare's work best illustrated organic form. Coleridge argued that 'nothing else could be substituted to excite the same sense of its exquisite propriety' (*MC,* 43) in Shakespearean poetry, which might also partially account for his anger at the alterations of Shakespeare's plays.

When Lamb considered the comic scenes in Shakespearean tragedy he found no inherent weakness in the juxtaposition of these different elements, but rather based his judgement on the manner in which the comic and tragic integrated in order to form a whole. Thus he turned away from such neo-classical ideas as the automatic objection to tragi-comedy, and showed an affinity with the principles advocated by Coleridge.

The poet or painter shews his art, when in the selection of these comic adjuncts he chooses such circumstances as shall relieve, contrast with, or fall into, without forming a violent opposition to, his principal object. Who sees not that the Grave-digger in *Hamlet,* the Fool in *Lear,* have a kind of correspondency to, and fall in with, the subjects which they seem to interrupt, while the comic stuff in *Venice Preserved,* and the doggrel nonsense of the Cook and his poisoning

115

associates in the *Rollo* of Beaumont and Fletcher, are pure, irrelevant, impertinent discords, – as bad as the quarrelling dog and cat under the table of the *Lord and the Disciples at Emmaus* of Titian? (I, 77).

This principle applied to painting as well as to drama; and Hogarth and Chaucer included 'many diverse yet co-operating materials' (I, 77) in their work. They maintained a unity. Just as Lamb did not believe that the comedy introduced by the Fool and the Grave-diggers interrupted the development of the drama, so Coleridge argued that Lear's Fool was 'brought into living connection with the pathos of the play, with the sufferings', and suggested that the Fool's 'grotesque prattling seems to indicate the dislocation of feeling that has begun and is to be continued' (*SC*, I, 63–4). Hamlet pointed to the significant contribution which comic elements might make to a play's total meaning when he warned actors against the false assumption that comic scenes in a tragic play offered an interlude for them to exercise their powers of comic display: 'and let those that play your clowns speak no more than is set down for them, for there be of them that will themselves laugh, to set on some quantity of barren spectators to laugh too, though in the mean time some necessary question of the play be then to be considered.' (III. ii. 37–42). Coleridge did not accept the idea of comic relief. If he believed that a comic scene did not relate to the play's development, as he felt to be the case of the Porter scene in *Macbeth*, he objected to it.

Lamb argued that the 'To be or not to be' soliloquy depended upon the harmony of its integration into the structure of the work. In a letter to Robert Lloyd on 18 November 1801 he wrote:

How beggarly and how bald do even Shakspeare's Princely Pieces look when thus violently divorced from *connection* and *circumstance!* When we meet with 'To be or not to be', or Jacques' moralisings upon the Deer, or Brutus and Cassius' quarrel and reconciliation – in an Enfield Speaker, or in Elegant Extracts, – how we stare, and will scarcely acknowledge to ourselves (what we are conscious we feel) that they are flat and have no power. (*Letters,* I, 285).

Once removed from its context it lost its value and vitality: 'It has been so handled and pawed about by declamatory boys and men, and torn so inhumanly from its living place and principle of continuity in the play, till it is become to me a perfect dead member' (I, 99). The opposition between 'living' and 'dead' emphasized Lamb's view of drama as progression and growth in accordance with the explanation of organic form given by Coleridge. In his notes to the *Specimens* Lamb wrote that, 'Shakspeare mingles every thing, he runs line into line, embarasses sentences and metaphors; before one idea has burst its shell, another is hatched and clamorous for disclosure' (IV, 341). Just as Coleridge regarded the Fool's relationship to *King Lear* as a 'living connection', so Lamb found the life of drama in its organic unity. The ability to develop the organic unity of a work depended upon the presence in the author of imagination, in the sense of Coleridge's definition of the secondary imagination in *Biographia Literaria:* 'It dissolves, dissipates, in order to recreate; or where this process is rendered impossible, yet still at all events it struggles to idealize and to unify. It is essentially *vital*, even as all objects (*as* objects) are essentially fixed and dead.'[11]

In his essay on the 'Sanity of True Genius' Lamb argued that the qualities of the secondary imagination existed in what he called the 'sanest writers'. These writers, the 'greatest wits' (and wit here referred to 'poetic talent') manifested an 'admirable balance of all the faculties'. They could write 'higher poetry' which was distinguished by 'a condition of exaltation' of which their readers had 'no parallel in their own experience, besides the spurious resemblance of it in dreams and fevers' (II, 187). The great wits could idealize life. As De Quincey argued, the life of Shakespeare's plays was 'treated upon a scale so sensibly different from the proper life of the spectator as to impress him profoundly with the feeling of its idealization. Shakespeare's tragic life is our own life exalted and selected'.[12] And in Coleridge's words the end of drama was that of 'imitating reality (objects, actions, or passions) under a semblance of reality' (*SC,* I, 199–200). Coleridge, Lamb and De Quincey all stressed in these quotations that art did not reproduce the reality of the spectator's life. This, Lamb argued, did not warrant the assumption that the poet indulged in 'a state of dreaminess and fever', for 'the true poet dreams being awake. He is not possessed by his subject, but has dominion over it'. Shakespeare could be 'content awhile to be mad with Lear' but he never let 'the reins of reason wholly go' (II, 187).

117

Lamb developed the essay by defining his conception of the distinction between the 'great and the little wits'. When the little wits

> wander ever so little from nature or actual existence, they lose themselves, and their readers. Their phantoms are lawless; their visions nightmares. They do not create, which implies shaping and consistency. Their imaginations are not active – for to be active is to call something into act and form – but passive, as men in sick dreams. For the super-natural, or something super-added to what we know of nature, they give you the plainly non-natural. (II, 188).

They lacked that shaping power of the imagination which Lamb as well as Coleridge valued as an essential quality of the best art. But, Lamb suggested, where the great wit 'seems most to recede from humanity, he will be found the truest to it. From beyond the scope of Nature if he summon possible existences, he subjugates them to the law of her consistency' (II, 187–8). He could present an imitation of supernatural existence which a reader found convincing because of the coherence of its presentation: 'His ideal tribes submit to policy . . . Caliban, the Witches, are as true to the laws of their own nature (ours with a difference), as Othello, Hamlet, and Macbeth' (II, 188). To borrow a phrase from the notes to the *Extracts from the Garrick Plays* this was 'not Nature's nature, but Imagination's substituted nature' (IV, 401). Lamb extended the contrast by comparing the descriptions by lesser wits of 'real and every day life, that which is before their eyes' with some of Spenser's description in the *Faery Queene*. Lamb argued that the lesser wits, although they referred to familiar sounding names and places, like 'Bath and Bond-street', bewildered their readers more than did Spenser, in whose *Faery Queene* 'we have names which announce fiction; and we have absolutely no place at all, for the things and persons of the Fairy Queen prate not of their "whereabout". But in their inner nature, and the law of their speech and actions, we are at home and upon acquainted ground' (II, 188–9). The work of the lesser wits proved that external resemblances to real life and existence bore only a limited significance in literature. Spenser's descriptions were remote from the reality of everyday life, but that did not mean that he had reproduced his dreams instead. Lamb rejected the idea that the poetic achievement of a true genius could be adequately characterized as *copy:* 'It is not enough to say that the whole episode is a copy of the mind's conceptions in sleep; it is, in some sort – but what a copy!' Lamb found the truth of Spenser's work in the coherence of its 'inner nature' rather than in the objective accuracy of its descriptions. Lamb applied this principle in his criticism of painting. The imaginative artist distorted real physical appearance in order to create his art and Lamb called this 'wise falsification'. The spectator's judgement did not object to what he saw. Similarly, in reading Spenser's *Faery Queene*, the judgement was 'neither able nor willing to detect the fallacy'. Coleridge made the same point when he wrote that Spenser 'has placed you in a dream, a charmed sleep, and you neither wish, nor have the power, to inquire where you are, or how you got there' (*MC,* 36). For Lamb this constituted 'a proof of that hidden sanity which still guides the poet in his widest seeming-aberrations' (II, 189). The imaginative artist endowed his work with a coherent form and compelled our judgements to regard his presentation as credible.

The critical principles which informed the essay on the 'Sanity of True genius' as well as the essays on painting were consistent with Lamb's comments on the stage presentation of Shakespearean tragedy. Lamb proposed that the effect which resulted from Shakespeare's introduction of supernatural agents in his tragedies was 'to give a wildness and a supernatural elevation to his scenes, as if to remove them still farther from that assimilation to common life in which their excellence is vulgarly supposed to consist' (I, 109). In reading Shakespeare, as with Spenser, the mind developed an absolute faith in the existence of the creations of the poet. Lamb admitted, in the essay on the 'Sanity of True Genius', that he did not understand by 'what subtle art of tracing the mental processes' a poet achieved such an effect, but the poet's 'subtile art' (I, 189) very evidently differed in an essential way from the theatre's attempt to emulate such an effect 'by the help of painted trees and caverns'. Lamb argued that, 'Contrary to the old saying, that "seeing is believing", the sight actually destroys the faith; . . . For this exposure of supernatural agents upon a stage is truly bringing in a candle to expose their own delusiveness' (I, 109). By trying 'to make all things natural' (I, 111) the stage abandoned 'that vantage-ground of abstraction' (I, 106) upon which the poet relied. Lamb found the contem-

119

porary theatre unsatisfactory as a medium for the poetic consciousness which created Shakespearean tragic heroes because
he desired the closest imaginative contact with the consciousness
of both the artist and the created character. Contemporary stage
productions impeded this aim, whereas reading, at least in Lamb's
experience, did not. Thus he wrote that 'the reading of a tragedy
is a fine abstraction' (I, 111). Lamb did not entertain the
impractical idea that the reading of a play could be the same as
a stage performance. He did not confound theatrical criticism and
the criticism of dramatic literature. The change of medium altered
the critic's response, and thus Lamb distinguished between the
reading and the staging of Shakespearean tragedy, but he did not
advocate one to the exclusion of the other.

NOTES
Introduction

1 G. D. Klingopulos, 'The Spirit of the Age in Prose', in *The Pelican Guide to English Literature: 5 From Blake to Byron*, ed. B. Ford (Harmondsworth: Penguin, 1957), 130-51 (p. 148, 145).

2 W. D. Howe, *Charles Lamb and His Friends* (Indianapolis: Bobbs-Merrill, 1944), p. 309.

3 W. K. Wimsatt, Jr., and C. Brooks, *Literary Criticism: A Short History* (London: Routledge, Kegan Paul, 1965), pp. 494-5. Rene Wellek also depreciated Lamb's Shakespearean criticism and wrote of it as a reaction 'to the deplorable tendencies of the theatre of his day' in *A History of Modern Criticism: 1750-1950*, 5 vols. (London: Johnathan Cape, 1955-66), II, 192. Other critics who have commented upon the relation between Lamb's criticism and the theatre in his time include J. W. Donohue Jr., John I. Ades, and Joan Coldwell. Donohue stressed Lamb's concern with 'the ideal performance' and rejected Wellek's assertion, in *Dramatic Character in the English Romantic Age* (Princeton: Princeton Univ. Press, 1970), pp. 282-3, 285. Ades saw Lamb struggling with 'two claims upon his critical judgement', firstly that 'the theatrical conditions of his time were simply inimical to the satisfactory playing of Shakespearean tragedy' and secondly that Shakespeare sometimes 'achieved such imaginative sublimity that no conceivable cast of actors could ever fulfill the poet's expectations'. Ades argued for the greater importance of the latter in determining Lamb's judgements. See 'Charles Lamb, Shakespeare, and the Early Nineteenth-century Theater', *PMLA*, 85 (1970), 514-26. Coldwell, in her comments on Lamb's analyses of Shakespearean characters, argued that the Romantic 'plea for a closet Shakespeare' related to the 'cult of the actor'. See 'The Playgoer as Critic: Charles Lamb on Shakespeare's Characters', *SQ*, 26 (1975), p. 184. What remains to be pointed out is the significance of Lamb's criticism of painting for a reading of his Shakespearean criticism.

4 *The Collected Writings of Thomas De Quincey*, ed. David Masson, 14 vols. (London: A. & C. Black, 1889-90), V, 236.

5 W. E. Houghton pointed this out in his article entitled 'Lamb's Criticism of Restoration Comedy', *ELH*, 10 (1943), 61-72.

6 *The Letters of Charles Lamb, to which are added those of his Sister, Mary Lamb*, ed. E. V. Lucas, 3 vols. (London: Dent; Methuen, 1935), II, 254. Further references are abbreviated *Letters* and follow quotations in the text.

7 *The Works of Charles and Mary Lamb*, ed. E. V. Lucas, 7 vols. (London: Methuen, 1903-05), II, 151. Further references follow quotations in the text.

8 For a discussion of 'sympathetic criticism' and 'imaginative identification' in Lamb's criticism, see Ades, p. 517.

9 Robert D. Frank, *Don't Call Me Gentle Charles!* (Corvallis: Oregon State Univ. Press, 1976), p. 13.

10 T. N. Talfourd, 'A Sketch of the Life of Charles Lamb: with Final Memorials', in *The Life, Letters and Writings of Charles Lamb,* ed. P. Fitzgerald, 6 vols. (London: John Slark, 1882), I, 129-30.

11 *Collected Letters of Samuel Taylor Coleridge,* ed. E. L. Griggs, 6 vols. (Oxford: Clarendon Press, 1956-71), I, 297, 588. George Whalley has commented upon Lamb's criticism of Coleridge in 'Coleridge's Debt to Charles Lamb', *Essays and Studies,* NS 11 (1958), 68-85.

12 *The Prose Works of William Wordsworth,* ed. W. J. B. Owen and Jane W. Smyser, 3 vols. (Oxford: Clarendon Press, 1974), I, 132.

13 *Prose Works of Wordsworth,* I, 131.

14 *Prose Works of Wordsworth,* I, 124, 126.

15 *The Life and Correspondence of Robert Southey,* ed. C. C. Southey, 6 vols. (London, 1849-50), II, 275.

16 *The Quarterly Review,* 6 (1811), 462-87 (p. 485). In a letter to Southey Gifford claimed that he was unaware of Lamb's personal situation and expressed regret for this remark. See *The Life and Correspondence of Southey,* V, 151n.

17 Talfourd, I, 268.

18 From B. Cornwall, *Charles Lamb: A Memoir* (London, 1866), and reprinted in *The Elian Miscellany: A Charles Lamb Anthology,* ed. S. M. Rich (London, 1931), p. 62.

Chapter I

1 Tate Wilkinson, *Memoirs of His Own Life,* 4 vols. (York, 1790), II, 139. See James J. Lynch, *Box Pit and Gallery. Stage and Society in Johnson's London* (Berkeley: Univ. of California Press, 1953), pp. 122-23. I am indebted to Lynch in this chapter.

2 *The Letters of David Garrick,* ed. David M. Little and George M. Kahrl, 3 vols. (London: Oxford Univ. Press, 1963), II, 549. Further references are abbreviated *LG* and follow quotations in the text.

3 Arthur Murphy, *The Life of David Garrick* (Dublin, 1801), p. 353. Lynch, p. 123.

4 Murphy, p. 354. See Lynch p. 124. John Weaver, a dancing-master at Drury Lane, first conceived the idea of pantomime. In 1716 he staged *The Loves of Mars and Venus* and *Perseus and Andromeda.*. John Rich popularized this form of entertainment. See John Jackson, *The History of the Scottish Stage* (Edinburgh, 1793), pp. 365-8, and A. M. Nagler, *A Source Book in Theatrical History* (New York: Dover Pulications, 1959), pp. 346-7.

5 John Genest, *Some Account of the English Stage from the Restoration in 1660 to 1830,* 10 vols. (Bath, 1832), VI, 569.

6 R. C. Rhodes, *Harlequin Sheridan* (Oxford: Blackwell, 1933), p. 53.

7 William Cooke, *Memoirs of Macklin* (London: James Asperne, 1804), pp. 44-5.

8 Thomas Davies, *Dramatic Miscellanies,* 3 vols. (London, 1783-4), II, 157. Lynch, p. 128.

9   Yvonne Ffrench, *Mrs Siddons: Tragic Actress* (1936; revised edition, London: Derek Verschoyle, 1954), p. 34.

10 Murphy, p. 133. Lynch, p. 127.

11 Murphy, p. 185, and p. 447.

12 Samuel Foote, *Examen of the New Comedy, call'd The Suspicious Husband with Some Observations upon our Dramatick Poetry and Authors; To which is added, A Word of Advice to Mr G--rr--ck* (London, 1747), p. 35. Mrs Frances Brooke, in a review of Spranger Barry's performance of Lear, in *The Old Maid, by Mary Singleton, Spinster,* no. 18, 13 March 1756; and quoted by R. G. Noyes, *The Thespian Mirror. Shakespeare in the Eighteenth-Century Novel,* Brown Univ. Studies, vol. 15 (Providence, R. I., 1953).

13 *Boswell's Life of Johnson,* ed. G. B. Hill, revised by L. F. Powell, 6 vols. (Oxford: Clarendon Press, 1934), II, 439. Lynch, p. 126.

14 See Walley C. Oulton, *A History of the Theatres of London,* 3 vols. (London, 1818), II, 20-30.

15 *English Review,* 1783, p. 73.

16 Rhodes, p. 101.

17 Lewis Gibbs, *Sheridan* (London: Dent, 1947), p. 55.

18 A. Nicoll, *A History of English Drama 1660-1900,* 6 vols. (Cambridge: The Univ. Press, 1952-9), III, 229.

19 *The Complete Works of William Hazlitt,* ed. P. P. Howe, 21 vols. (London: Dent, 1930-4), V, 237. Further references follow quotations in the text.

20 See Ffrench, p. 156.

21 *The Journal of William Charles Macready,* ed. J. C. Trewin (London: Longmans, 1967), p. 189.

22 *Letters of Coleridge,* I, 379.

23 *The Life of Thomas Holcroft written by Himself,* ed. E. Colby, 2 vols. (London: Constable, 1925), I, 153-4. See A. Thaler, 'Strolling Players and Provincial Drama after Shakespeare', *PMLA,* 37 (1922), 243-80.

24 See Herschel Baker, 'Strolling Actors in Enghteenth-Century England', *University of Texas Studies in English,* 20 (1941), 100-20.

25 John Doran, *Their Majesties' Servants: Annals of the English Stage, from Thomas Betterton to Edmund Kean. Actors, Authors, Audiences,* 2 vols. (London: Wm. H. Allen, 1864), II, 369.

26 See H. N. Hillebrand, *Edmund Kean* (New York: Columbia Univ. Press, 1933), p. 151 and p. 138; and A. S. Downer, *The Eminent Tragedian. William Charles Macready* (London: Oxford Univ. Press, 1966), p. 50.

27 W. Archer, *William Charles Macready* (London: Kegan Paul, Trench, Trübner, 1890), p. 210.

28 R. B. Peake, *Memoirs of the Colman Family,* 2 vols. (London, 1841), II, 414.

29 See Peake, II, 237.

30 See Ffrench, p. 151.
31 *Journal of Macready*, pp. 12-13.
32 See Lily B. Campbell, 'The Rise of a Theory of Stage Presentation in England during the Eighteenth Century', *PMLA*, 32 (1917), 163-200.
33 Cooke, pp. 98-9. Quoted by Campbell.
34 Alvin Whitley, 'Hazlitt and the Theater', *University of Texas Studies in English*, 34 (1955), 67-100 (p. 77).
35 *The Autobiography of Leigh Hunt*, ed. J. E. Morpurgo (London: Cresset Press, 1949), p. 132, 157.
36 *Specimens of the Table Talk of Samuel Taylor Coleridge* (London, 1865), p. 14.
37 See *Journal of Macready*, p. 73.
38 Spoken by Garrick on the opening of Drury Lane in 1747. *The Yale Edition of the Works of Samuel Johnson*, 8 vols. (New Haven and London: Yale Univ. Press, 1958-68), VI *Poems* (1964), ed. E. L. McAdam, Jr., with George Milne, p. 89.
39 See Nicoll, III, 5-7.
40 Peake, II, 363. Colman was replying to Arnold's assertion that 'there was no tumult or disorder (in the theatre) which I was told almost never took place but when something was radically wrong'. p. 360.
41 *The Autobiography of Leigh Hunt*, p. 155.
42 See Nicoll, III, 17-19.
43 See Charles H. Gray, *Theatrical Criticism in London to 1795*, Columbia Univ. Studies in English and Comparative Literature (New York, 1931), p. 196.
44 *The Yale Johnson*, VII and VIII, *Johnson on Shakespeare* (1968), ed. A. Sherbo, VIII, 704, and VII, 71. See also B. H. Bronson's introduction VII, xxxiii-iv.
45 See Nicoll, IV, 52.
46 *The Bee*, No. VIII, 24 November 1759, in *Collected Works of Oliver Goldsmith*, ed. A. Friedman, 5 vols. (Oxford: Clarendon Press, 1966), I, 508.
47 *Works of Goldsmith*, I, 11.
48 See Peake, I, 272 and 273.
49 *Works of Goldsmith*, I, 328 and 330.
50 See Peake, I, 274.
51 Leigh Hunt, *Critical Essays on the Performers of the London Theatres* (London: John Hunt, 1807), p. v.
52 Peake, II, 239-40.
53 *Marino Faliero, Doge of Venice. An Historical Tragedy, in Five Acts* (1821), Preface, p. xviii. Quoted by Donohue, pp. 157-8. Donohue comments on *The Cenci*, pp. 157-86.
54 *The Complete Poetical Works of Percy Bysshe Shelley*, ed. T. A. Hutchinson. A new edition corrected by G. M. Matthews (London: Oxford Univ. Press, 1970), p. 337.
55 *Poetical Works of Shelley*, p. 336.

Chapter II

1 F. V. Morley, *Lamb before Elia* (London: Johnathan Cape, 1932), p. 270.
2 James Shokhoff, 'Charles Lamb and the Elizabethan Dramatists: A Reassessment', *The Wordsworth Circle*, 4 (1973), 3-11 (p. 8). See also E. R. Wasserman, 'The Scholarly Origin of the Elizabethan Revival', *ELH*, 4 (1937), 213-43, and *Elizabethan Poetry in the Eighteenth Century* (Urbana, 1947); R. D. Williams, 'Antiquarian Interest in the Elizabethan Drama before Lamb', *PMLA*, 53 (1938), 434-44; F. S. Boas, 'Charles Lamb and the Elizabethan Dramatists', *ES*, 29 (1943), 62-81; R. C. Bald, 'Charles Lamb and the Elizabethans', in *Studies in Honor of A. H. R. Fairchild*, ed. C. T. Prouty, *University of Missouri Studies*, vol. XXI, no. 1 (1946), 169-74.
3 D. S. Perry, 'Hazlitt, Lamb and the Drama' (Ph. D. diss. Princeton University, 1966), p. 376.
4 See Shokhoff, p. 7.
5 Williams, p. 444.
6 Shokhoff, pp. 3-4.
7 For detailed discussion see Perry, pp. 382-403.
8 Klingopulos, p. 147. A. Swinburne, *The Age of Shakespeare* (London, 1908), 'Dedication'.
9 *Elegant Extracts*, ed. Vicesimus Knox (London, 1796). For Lamb's comment on Knox, see p. 38.
10 *Prose Works of Wordsworth*, I, 128.
11 *The Monthly Review*, 58 (1809), 349-56.
12 G. Watson, *The Literary Critics* (Harmondsworth: Penguin, 1962), p. 132.
13 See note 16 to the Introduction.
14 Wimsatt and Brooks, pp. 494-5. Subsequent quotations from Wimsatt and Brooks are from these pages.
15 Oscar Wilde, 'The Critic as Artist', in *Intentions* (London, 1913), p. 194.
16 *William Shakespeare: The Complete Works*, ed. P. Alexander (London and Glasgow: Collins, 1951), *Hamlet*, III. ii. 385. Further references to Shakespeare are to this edition and follow quotations in the text.
17 *Personal Recollections of Lamb, Hazlitt, and Others*, ed. R. H. Stoddard (New York, 1875), p. 41.
18 *Letters of John Keats, 1814-21*, ed. Hyder E. Rollins (Cambridge, Mass: Harvard Univ. Press, 1958), II, 213. See Roy Park, *Hazlitt and the Spirit of the Age* (Oxford: Clarendon Press, 1971), pp. 32-8.
19 Perry, pp. 315-19.
20 Northrop Frye, *Anatomy of Criticism* (Princeton: Princeton Univ. Press, 1957), p. 8.
21 *Letters of Coleridge*, III, 59 and I, 588.

Chapter III

1 J. E. Morpurgo, ed., *Charles Lamb and Elia* (Harmondsworth: Penguin, 1948), p. 18.

2 See also N. J. Lott, 'The Tragedies of Scott, Lamb, and Coleridge: Their Elizabethan Heritage' (Ph. D. diss., University of Southern Mississippi, 1971), p. 65.

3 F. Fergusson, *The Idea of a Theater* (Princeton: Princeton Univ. Press, 1949), p. 50.

4 *New Letters of Robert Southey,* ed. K. Curry, 2 vols. (New York: Columbia Univ. Press, 1965), I, 316.

5 Richard Haven, 'The Romantic Art of Charles Lamb', *ELH,* 30 (1963), 137-46 (pp. 146, 137, 138).

6 See Fred V. Randel, *The World of Elia* (Port Washington: Kennikat Press, 1975), p. 21; *Collected Writings of De Quincey,* V, 231-6, III, 88.

7 *Table Talk,* pp. 213-14.

8 See note 4.

9 'Rymer on Tragedy', in *The Retrospective Review,* 1 (1820), 1-16 (p. 15).

10 *Prose Works of Wordsworth,* I, 131.

11 See Hazlitt, XI, 182-3.

12 *Biographia Literaria,* ed. J. Shawcross, 2 vols. (Oxford: Clarendon Press, 1907), I, 4.

13 See also Lott, p. 65: 'when Lamb wrote *John Woodvil,* not only was his head full of the poetry of Shakespeare, Beaumont and Fletcher, and Marlowe, but he also had apparently concluded that the only worthy object of tragedy is the "internal workings" of great minds'.

14 Nicoll, III, 68.

15 Lott, pp. 78-9.

16 See Lucas, V, 350.

17 *Selections from the Letters of Robert Southey,* ed. J. W. Warter, 4 vols. (London, 1856), I, 297; *Letters of Coleridge,* I, 653-4; *New Letters of Robert Southey,* I, 315-16; *The Edinburgh Review* 2 (1803), 90-6.

18 *The Monthly Mirror,* 13 (April, 1802); *The Monthly Review,* 40 (1803), 442-3; *The Annual Review,* 1 (1802), 688-92; *The British Critic,* 19 (1802), 646-7; *The Monthly Magazine,* Suppl. v14 (1803), 600.

19 W. R. Nethery, *Mr H in America or, Anonymous Redivivus* (Los Angeles, 1956).

20 Jules Derocquigny, *Charles Lamb: sa vie et ses oeuvres* (Lille: The University, 1904), p. 370.

21 *The Dramatic Essays of Charles Lamb,* ed. Brander Matthews (London: Chatto and Windus, 1891), p. 27. Matthews also stressed the 'literary' quality of the play.

22 Nicoll, IV, 123-4.

23 *The Works of Lord Byron, Letters and Journals,* ed. R. E. Prothero, 6 vols (London: John Murray, 1898-1901), IV, 71-2.

24 J. B. Priestley, *The Art of the Dramatist* (London: Heinemann, 1957), p. 66.

25 'The Confidant', in George Crabbe, *Tales, 1812 and Other Selected Poems,* ed. H. Mills (Cambridge: The Univ. Press, 1967), 353-5. Further references follow quotations in the text.

26 *The Works of Charles Lamb,* ed. W. Macdonald, 12 vols. (London: J. M. Dent, 1903), V, 246.

27 R. D. Altick, *The English Common Reader* (Chicago: Chicago Univ. Press, 1957), p. 139.

Chapter IV

1 See Houghton, p. 68. Houghton also commented on the relationship between 'Stage Illusion' and theories of acting but he denied that the latter essay exercised a 'bearing on his [Lamb's] theory of artificial comedy, since it concerns only the technique of acting' (p. 72).

2 Sylvan Barnet, 'Charles Lamb's Contribution to the Theory of Dramatic Illusion', *PMLA,* 69 (1954), 1150-9.

3 William Congreve, *The Way of the World,* ed. John Barnard, The Fountainwell Drama Texts (Edinburgh: Oliver and Boyd, 1972), p. 16.

4 Northrop Frye, *Fools of Time: studies in Shakespearean Tragedy* (London: Oxford Univ. Press; Toronto: Toronto Univ. Press, 1967), pp. 3-4.

5 S. Barnet, 'Charles Lamb and the Tragic Malvolio', *PQ,* 33 (1954), 178-88 (p. 187).

6 M. J. Young, *Memoirs of Mrs Crouch,* 2 vols. (London, 1806), II, 35. Quoted by Barnet, *PQ,* p. 184.

7 Barnet, *PQ,* p. 185. John Taylor, *Records of My Life,* 2 vols. (London, 1832), I, 431, and II, 143. Genest, VII, 252. Colman, II, 7.

8 Colman, II, 7.

9 John Adolphus, *Memoirs of John Bannister,* 2 vols. (London, 1839), I, 129. Quoted by Barnet, *PQ,* p. 184.

10 Adolphus, I, 129.

11 James Boaden, *The Life of Mrs Jordan,* 2 vols. (London, 1831), I, 24. Quoted by Barnet, *PQ,* p. 184, and p. 186.

12 Park, p. 142.

13 Leigh Hunt, *Critical Essays on the Performers of the London Theatres,* p. 32, and 31.

14 'Charles Lamb on the New Comedy, "Debtor and Creditor"', in Edmund Blunden, *Leigh Hunt's "Examiner" Examined 1808-25* (London: Cobden-Sanderson, 1928), p. 249.

15 *Leigh Hunt's Dramatic Criticism: 1808-1831,* ed. L. W. and C. W. Houtchens (New York: Columbia Univ. Press, 1949), p. 90.

16 In *Letters,* III, 137, Lucas has *analysis* and not *analogies.* See G. L. Barnett, 'Corrections in the Text of Lamb's Letters', *HLQ,* 18 (1955), p. 155.

17 G. C. D. Odell, *Shakespeare From Betterton to Irving*, 2 vols. (London: Constable, 1921), II, 135.

18 *Coleridge's Miscellaneous Criticism*, ed. T. M. Raysor (London: Constable, 1936), p. 89. Further references are abbreviated *MC* and follow quotations in the text.

19 T. B. Macaulay, *Critical and Historical Essays*, 2 vols. (London: Dent, 1967), II, 418.

20 Houghton, p. 63.

21 E. E. Stoll, *Shakespeare Studies* (New York, 1927), p. 46.

Chapter V

1 *Boswell's Life of Johnson*, II, 92; A. C. Bradley, *Shakespearean Tragedy* (London: Macmillan, 1904), p. 248; T. S. Eliot, *Selected Essays* (New York, 1932), p. 95.

2 *Blackwood's Edinburgh Magazine*, 3 (1818), 599-610 (p. 607).

3 Fanny Kemble, *Records of a Childhood* (New York, 1883), p. 249.

4 *Coleridge's Shakespearean Criticism*, ed. T. M. Raysor, 2 vols. (London: Constable, 1930), I, 137. Further references are abbreviated *SC* and follow quotations in the text.

5 *S. T. Coleridge: Treatise on Method as published in the Encyclopaedia Metropolitana*, ed. A. D. Snyder (London: Constable, 1934), p. 62.

6 See M. M. Badawi, *Coleridge: Critic of Shakespeare* (Cambridge: The University Press, 1973), p. 59; and Park, p. 125: 'Like Hazlitt and Jeffrey, he [Coleridge] did not demand the object in all its vivid visual detail, but the object as symbol – created not by observation alone, but by the union of meditation and observation'. Park commented on the anti-pictorialism of Coleridge and Hazlitt, especially in his fifth chapter. See also J. R. de J. Jackson, 'Coleridge on Dramatic Illusion and Spectacle in the Performance of Shakespeare's Plays', *MP*, 62 (1964), 13-21.

7 S. M. Tave, *The Amiable Humorist* (Chicago: Chicago Univ. Press, 1960), p. 203.

8 *Letters of Coleridge*, III, 501.

9 F. Gentleman, *The Dramatic Censor*, 2 vols. (London, 1770), I, 59.

10 *The Monthly Mirror*, 10 (1800), p. 319: 'Mr Cooke has introduced three lines from the *Third Part of King Henry VI* which are very suitable to his manner of playing the part.

> Why I can smile, and murder while I smile,
> And cry content to that which grieves my heart;
> And wet my cheeks with artificial tears,
> And frame my face to all occasions.

. . . We have seen *Richard* rendered more awful and terrific, but never more thoroughly detestable'.

11 *Biographia Literaria*, I, 202.

12 *Collected Writings of De Quincey*, X, 347.

Index

Ades, John I., 121n
Adolphus, John, 80, 81, 127n
Aiken (Aickin), 81
Albion, 16
Alexander, P., 125n
Altick, R. D., 72, 127n
American Monthly Magazine and Critical Review, 64
Annual Review, 63, 126n
Archer, W., 26, 123n
Arnold, Samuel, 20, 124n
Athenaeum, 82
Atlas, 72

Badawi, M. M., 128n
Baker, Herschel, 123n
Bald, R. C., 125n
Bannister, John, 73, 74, 82, 86, 87, 91, 92, 127n
Barnard, John, 127n
Barnet, Sylvan, 78, 79-81, 127n
Barnett, G. L., 127n
Barry, Spranger, 22, 123n
Barton, Bernard, 14, 50, 55
Beard, John, 20, 22
Beaumont, Francis, 11, 32, 38, 39, 40, 58, 116, 126n
Bensley, Robert, 8, 73, 75-82
Bentham, J., 72
Betterton, Thomas, 107, 123n, 128n
Blackwood's Edinburgh Magazine, 55, 68, 98, 128n
Blunden, Edmund, 127n
Boaden, James, 80, 81, 127n
Boas, F. S., 125n
Booth, Junius Brutus, 26
Boswell, James, 97, 123n, 128n
Boydell, Alderman, 105
Boyer, Rev. James, 59
Bradley, A. C., 97, 128n
British Critic, 63, 126n
Bronson, B. H., 124n
Brooks, Cleanth, 7, 50, 51, 121n, 125n
Brooke, Mrs Frances, 21, 123n

Brown, Thomas, 63
Bullen, A. H., 39
Bunn, Alfred, 24
Burnet, Gilbert, 65, 95
Burrell, Miss, 9
Byron, Lord, 14, 15, 35-6 38, 67, 126n

Campbell, Lily B., 124n
Canning, George, 16
Castlereagh, 16
Castles, 16
Champion, 16
Chapman, George, 43
Charron, Sieur de, 90
Chaucer, Geoffrey, 56, 116
Chesterfield, Lord, 34
Cibber, Colley, 106
Clarkson, Mrs, 66
Colby, E., 123n
Coldwell, Joan, 121n
Coleridge, S. T., 7, 9-15 passim, 23, 24, 30, 38, 45, 52-63 passim, 97, 100-28 passim
Collins, John Churton, 39
Colman, George, 34
Colman, the Younger, George, 20, 27, 31, 35, 63, 80, 124n, 127n
Congreve, William, 49, 64, 77, 87, 88, 92, 94, 95, 127n
Cooke, G. F., 113, 128n
Cooke, William, 20, 29, 123n, 124n
Cornwall, Barry. See Procter, B. W.
Cottle, Joseph, 11
Crabbe, George, 56, 69-72, 127n
Crouch, Mrs, 79, 127n
Curry, Kenneth, 126n

Davenport, Robert, 40
Davies, Thomas, 21, 123n
Da Vinci, Leonardo, 104
Dekker, Thomas, 45, 47, 48
De Quincey, Thomas, 7, 57, 58, 117, 121n, 126n, 128n
Derocquigny, Jules, 65, 126n

Dibdin, Charles, 22
Dibdin, T. J., 35
Dodd, James William, 8, 30, 82-4, 86
Dodsley, Robert, 39
Donohue, J. W., Jr., 121n, 124n
Doran, John, 26, 123n
Downer, A. S., 123n
Dowton, W., 85, 86
Dryden, John, 52, 95
Dyce, Alexander, 39-40

Edinburgh Review, 63, 126n
Edwards, George, 16
Eliot, T. S., 97, 128n
Elliston, R. W., 9
Emery, John, 74, 75
English Review, 23, 123n
Examiner, 16, 86, 87, 89, 127n

Fairchild, A. H. R., 125n
Farquhar, George, 64
Felix Farley's Bristol Journal, 87
Fergusson, Francis, 56, 126n
Ferriar, John, 63
Ffrench, Yvonne, 21, 123n, 124n
Field, Barron, 39, 88
Fitzgerald, Percy, 122n
Fleetwood, Charles, 30, 31
Fletcher, John, 11, 32, 38, 39, 40, 43, 47, 49, 58, 116, 126n
Foote, Samuel, 21, 123n
Ford, John, 14, 39, 47, 60
Frank, Robert D., 9, 122n
Frye, Northrop, 53, 79, 125n, 127n
Fuseli, Henry, 83, 105

Garrick, David, 19-35 passim, 99, 100, 106, 108, 110, 122n, 124n
Garrick, Mrs Eva, 27
Gazetteer, 81
Genest, John, 20, 80, 122n, 127n
Gentleman, Francis, 128n
Gentleman's Magazine, 80
George III, 17
George IV (Prince Regent), 16, 17
Gibbon, Edward, 65
Gibbs, Lewis, pseud. (Joseph Walter Cove) 22, 123n

Gifford, William, 14, 16, 17, 47, 52, 122n
Godwin, William, 11, 53, 59, 63, 93
Goethe, J. W., 61
Goldsmith, Oliver, 19, 33, 34, 35, 36, 124n
Gray, Charles H., 124n
Griggs, E. L., 122n
Grimaldi, Joseph, 30

Harcourt, Lady, 24
Harris, Thomas, 36
Haven, Richard, 57, 126n
Hazlitt, William, 13, 15, 23, 24, 25, 29, 30, 39, 40, 43, 50, 52, 53, 59, 72, 75, 76, 78, 82-88 passim, 97, 102, 105, 108, 109, 112, 113, 123n, 125n, 126n, 128n
Henderson, John, 22, 28
Heywood, Thomas, 10, 45, 112
Hill, G. B., 123n
Hillebrand, H. N., 123n
Hilson, Mr, 64
Hoadly, Rev. John, 32
Hogarth, William, 40, 41, 56, 100, 102, 116,
Holcroft, Thomas, 25, 31, 123n
Holland, Henry, 23
Home, John, 33
Homer, 76
Hone, William, 55
Houghton, W. E., 73, 95, 121n, 127n, 128n
Houtchens, L. W. & C. W., 127n
Howe, P. P., 123n
Howe, W. D., 7, 121n
Hume, David, 103
Hunt, John, 31
Hunt, J. H. Leigh, 14, 16, 29, 30, 31, 35, 72, 85, 86, 88, 89, 124n, 127n
Hutchinson, T. A., 124n

Irving, Sir Henry, 128n

Jackson, John, 122n
Jackson, J. R. de J., 128n
Jeffrey, Francis, 128n
Johnson, Samuel, 22, 30, 32, 33, 97, 123n, 124n, 128n

Jonson, Ben, 39, 101
Jordan, Mrs, 8, 25, 27, 73, 82, 85, 87-90, 91, 127n

Kahrl, G. M., 20, 122n
Kean, Edmund, 23, 26, 29, 30, 75-6, 83, 123n
Keats, John, 52, 53, 125n
Kelly, Fanny, 8, 9, 73, 82, 85-90, 91
Kemble, Charles, 9, 69
Kemble, Fanny, 99, 128n
Kemble, John Philip, 23, 24, 25, 26, 29, 30, 31, 35, 63, 81, 113
Kemble, Roger, 25
Kenney, James, 9
King, Thomas, 23, 26, 92
Klingopulos, G. D., 7, 40, 121n, 125n
Knowles, James Sheridan, 9
Knox, Vicesimus, 38, 45, 125n
Kotzebue, A. F. F. von, 61

Lamb, Charles, on acting, artificial and natural, 73-96 passim; as actor, 8; 'On the Artificial Comedy of the Last Century', 8, 47, 49, 64, 73, 87, 88, 90, 91-6, 102, 111; 'Barrenness of the Imaginative Faculty in the Productions of Modern Art', 42, 100, 103-05; on Barton, 14; on Beaumont and Fletcher, 38; on Bensley, 75-82; on Bryon, 14-15, 38; on Chapman, 43; on Chaucer, 56, 116; 'Christ's Hospital Five and Thirty Years Ago', 9; on Coleridge,10-13, 15, 38; Coleridge on Lamb's taste, 53; 'Confessions of a Drunkard', 14; on Congreve, 49, 94; and Crabbe's 'The Confidant', 69-72; criticism, alleged conventional piety of, 47-50; criticism, alleged impressionism of, 50-3; criticism, not systematic, 52-3; criticism, ungentle, 13-17; 'On the Custom of Hissing at the Theatre', 67-8; on decorum, 37, 40-3, 49; on Dekker, 45, 47-8; on Dodd, 82-4; on drama, contemporary, 43-7 passim; on Dryden,

52; Elia and *Essays of Elia*, 8, 9, 13, 50, 57, 82; Elia, De Quincey on, 57-8; Elia, Southey on, 50; Elizabethan and Jacobean dramatists, 37-53, 55, (their moral sense, 43-5, 50); *Extracts from the Garrick Plays*, 7, 10, 37-50 passim, 55, 82, 112, 118; on Fletcher, 43, 47, 49; on Ford, 47, 60; friendship, 13; on gentle, 9-10; 'The Godlike', 17; and Hazlitt, 13, 39; on Heywood, 10, 45; on Hogarth and 'On the Genius and Character of Hogarth', 40, 41, 56, 100-03, 116; and Leigh Hunt, 13-14, 16; *John Woodvil*, 55-63, 65, 69, 71, 72; and Kean's Iago, 75-6; and Fanny Kelly, 8, 9, 73, 82, 85-90, 91; on J. P. Kemble, 81; on Knox, 38, 45; and Charles Lloyd, 13; on Marlowe, 47; on Massinger, 38, 47-8; on Middleton, 44, 52; on Milton, 49, 58; *Mr H*, 64-7, 69; Munden, 9, 82-85; on Otway, 38; on painting, 100-05, 119; *The Pawnbroker's Daughter*, 64, 65, 68; on Peele, 48-9; political satire, 15-17; on Raphael, 42; on Rowley, 44; 'Sanity of True Genius', 117-19; on Shakespeare and 'On the Tragedies of Shakspeare', 7, 8, 10, 15, 43, 44, 46, 50, 56, 59, 61, 64, 69, 87, 88, 90, 97-120, and *All's Well*, (Helena), 40, 41; *As You Like It*, and *John Woodvil*, 62-3, Jacques, 116; *Cymbeline* (Imogen and Posthumus), 105, 108; *Hamlet*, 51-2, 97, 107, 110, 114, 115, 116, 118; *Henry IV* (Falstaff), 105; *Julius Caesar* (Brutus and Cassius), 116; *King Lear*, 42-3, 106-07, 112-13, 115, 116, 117; *Macbeth*, 52, 110, 111, 113, 118;

The Merchant of Venice and *The Pawnbroker's Daughter*, 68;
A Midsummer Night's Dream, 49, 58, 75;
Much Ado, 14;
Othello, 60, 75-6, 94, 105, 108, 110, 111, 118;
Richard III, 40-1, 99, 111, 112, 113-14;
Romeo and Juliet, 105, 108, 109;
The Tempest, 48, 95, 118;
Twelfth Night, 62, 75-82, 89-90;
on Shelley, 14-15; on Sidney's *Arcadia*, 40, 41, 49; 'On Some of the Old Actors', 62, 75-85, 91-2; on Southey, 11, 13; *Specimens*, 7, 14, 37-53, 55, 60, 61, 64, 67, 82, 114, 117; on Spenser, 117-19; 'Stage Illusion', 8, 73-5, 88, 91; on subjectivity of creative process, 37, 40-2; on theatre audiences, contemporary, 46-7, 49, 59; on Tourneur, 51-2; 'The Triumph of the Whale', 16; on Webster, 42, 45, 47; *The Wife's Trial*, 55, 56, 68-72; on Wordsworth, 14, 40, 41, 45, 46
Lamb, Mary, 9, 12, 66
Lewis, Matthew, 24
Lewis, W. T., 35
Liston, John, 9, 30
Little, D. M., 122n
Lloyd, Charles, 13,
Lloyd, Robert, 40, 112, 116
London Chronicle, 31
London Daily Advertiser and Literary Gazette, 32
London Magazine, 13
Lott, N. J., 62, 126n
Love, James, 25
Lucas, E. V., 86, 121n, 126n, 127n
Lynch, J. J., 19, 26, 122n, 123n

McAdam, Jr., E. L., 124n
Macaulay, T. B., 95, 128n
Macdonald, W., 72, 127n

Mackintosh, Sir James, 15
Macklin, Charles, 28, 29
Macready, William Charles, 9, 24, 26, 27, 28, 30, 123n, 124n
Maddox, Anthony, 21
Malthus, Thomas, 72
Mandeville, Bernard de, 72
Manning, Thomas, 16, 38, 60, 63, 64, 65
Marlowe, Christopher, 47, 126n
Massinger, Philip, 38, 39, 47, 48, 58
Masson, David, 121n
Mathews, Charles, 9
Matthews, Brander, 66, 126n
Matthews, G. M., 124n
Michelangelo, 83
Middleton, Thomas, 44, 52
Mills, H., 127n
Milne, George, 124n
Milton, John, 49, 58
Montaigne, 90
Monthly Magazine, 63, 126n
Monthly Mirror, 63, 126n 128n
Monthly Review, 33, 63, 125n 126n
Morley, F. V., 37, 125n
Morning Chronicle, 16
Morning Chronicle, and London Advertiser, 81
Morpurgo, J. E., 55, 124n, 126n
Munden, J. S., 8, 9, 30, 35, 82-5, 88
Murphy, Arthur, 20, 122n, 123n

Nagler, A. M., 122n
Nethery, W. R., 64, 126n
News, 31
Nicoll, Allardyce, 61, 66, 123n, 124n, 126n
Northcote, James, 105
Noyes, R. G., 123n

Odell, G. C. D., 128n
Oliver, 16
O'Neill, Eliza, 36
Opie, John, 105
Otway, Thomas, 38, 115
Oulton, W. C., 123n
Owen, W. J. B., 122n

Paine, Thomas, 31

Palmer, John, 73, 91-2, 95-6
Park, Roy, 83, 125n, 127n, 128n
Parsons, William, 84, 86
Patmore, P. G., 52, 69
Payne, J. H., 9
Peake, R. B., 26, 27, 123n, 124n
Peele, George, 48
Perry, D. S., 38, 53, 125n
Perry, Mr, 16
Powell, L. F., 123n
Powell, William, 28
Priestley, J. B., 67, 127n
Procter, B. W., 122n
Prompter, 97-8
Prothero, R. E., 126n
Prouty, C. T., 125n
Public Advertiser, 93
Public Ledger, 32

Quarterly Review, 13, 14, 122n

Racine, Jean, 56
Randel, F. V., 57, 126n
Raphael, 42
Raysor, T. M., 128n
Reflector, 100
Retrospective Review, 58-9
Reynolds, Frederick, 33, 35, 90
Reynolds, Sir Joshua, 35
Rhodes, R. Crompton, 20, 122n, 123n
Rich, John, 20, 22, 29
Rich, S. M., 122n
Rickman, John, 56, 60, 61
Robertson, Henry, 9
Robertson, William, 65
Rogers, Samuel, 105
Rollins, Hyder E., 125n
Rowley, William, 44
Rymer, Thomas, 126n

Schiller, J. C. F. von, 61
Scott, Sir Walter, 126n
Shadwell, Thomas, 107
Shawcross, John, 126n
Shelley, P. B., 14, 15, 35, 36, 124n
Shelley, Mrs Mary, 56
Shepherd, R. H., 39
Sherbo, A., 124n

Sheridan, Mrs Elizabeth, 20
Sheridan R. B., 19, 22, 23, 24, 27, 33, 87, 88, 91, 92
Shokhoff, James, 37-8, 39, 125n
Siddons, Sarah, 23, 24, 25, 27, 29, 30, 110, 113,
Sidney, Sir Philip, 40, 41, 49
Smith, Adam, 103
Smith, William, 22, 26
Smollett, Tobias, 34
Smyser, J. W., 122n
Snyder, A. D., 128n
Southey, C. C., 122n
Southey, Robert, 7, 10, 11, 13, 14, 50, 53, 55, 56, 58, 63, 122n, 126n
Spenser, Edmund, 118-19
Stoddard, R. H., 125n
Stoll, E.E., 95, 128n
Swinburne, A. C., 40, 125n

Talfourd, T. N., 9, 15, 26, 122n
Tate, Nahum, 21, 22, 32, 42, 43, 106, 107
Tave, S. M., 103, 128n
Taylor, John, 80, 127n
Thaler, A., 123n
Thomson, James, 68
Titian, 57, 116
Tourneur, Cyril, 51, 52
Tree, Maria, 90
Trewin, J. C., 123n

Vandyke, 83

Warter, J. W., 126n
Wassermann, E. R., 39, 125n
Watson, George, 47, 125n
Weaver, John, 122n
Webster, John, 42, 45, 47, 67
Wellek, Rene, 121n
West, 105
Whalley, George, 122n
Whitley, Alvin, 29, 124n
Wilde, Oscar, 50, 125n
Wilkinson, Tate, 19, 25, 122n
Williams, R. D., 39, 125n
Wilson, John, 98-9
Wimsatt, W. K., 7, 50, 51, 121n, 125n

Wither, George, 58
Wood, William, 64
Wordsworth, Dorothy, 9
Wordsworth, William, 10, 11, 12, 14, 15, 24, 40, 41, 45, 46, 57, 63, 66, 122n, 125n, 126n

Wycherley, William, 64, 95

Yates, Mrs Mary Ann, 31
Yorke, Charles, 19
Young, Mrs, 79-80, 127n